YOU CAN MAKE IT!

A Story of Redemption, Grace and Perseverance

I dedicate this book to my Heavenly Father who has sustained me and kept me along this life's journey, who has saved my soul and redeemed me when I could have died in my sins. Also to my husband who has walked alongside this path with me. To my precious daughter, Kayla, you are a gift straight from Heaven that gives me a reason to wake up each day with purpose.

Table of Contents

TESTIMONIALS

"[I] read your book cover to cover through my tears. No child should have to endure what you went through. But in your teenage years you were led to Christ and you were transformed from a sad desperate soul into the most loving Christ-like young woman I have ever known. You have continued faithfully to serve God and He has blessed you for your faithfulness. Thank you for writing this book. It will show others the mighty power that is in Christ, His arms are wide open for anyone who will put their trust in Him. He can take a broken soul and make him (her) whole again.

-Aunt Barbara

It has been my privilege to have known Diana these past 15 years. She is truly a light in this dark world, with her contagious smile and joyful spirit she illuminates where ever she is. Her road has been harder than a lot of folks, but God has brought her through with a stronger love for Him and for others. I am so proud to call you friend, love always!

- Robin Baker

"Diana, I just finished your story. Let me just say it touched me in so many ways and I never knew we both grieve the same way-by staying busy. There isn't a thing I would add to your story, it is perfect. Get it published ASAP because I know of several that would enjoy and benefit from reading it. You are an amazing friend, mother, and wife and daughter. You were always there for your parents, and I know they are proud of the woman you have become. We are so grateful for wonderful friends like you, James, and Kayla. Even though we have outgrown our home, we stay because of all our neighbors, Love you!"

-ChelseaNash

"Hey..... I enjoyed your writings. You never know all a person goes through in life!! We all have a story....I am happy that you listened, and got this done. God always talks to us, and lets us know what He wants, or expects from us. I am sure you will continue to obey God, and He will continue to help you overcome all the day to day tragedies, and uncertainties. You have certainly overcome a lot in your past, and in the present. Your belief in God is certainly being noticed by Him. Love you! Keep doing what you believe in! You are reaping from your faithfulness."

-Melanie

"You do have a story tell. This has given me a new awareness to be sensitive to the needs of others. When we meet people, we never know what they are going through. We smile and say hi, but we are crying on the inside wondering does anyone really care. I ask the Holy Spirit to help me to be more sensitive or spiritually aware of others and their needs. I believe that the Lord will give you the desires of your heart and that your life will touch many people. May the Lord bless the works of your hands."

Your brother in Christ

"When my wife and I first met Diana it was through a family that had made a difference in her life. Diana's story tells how the Lord uses people to touch other people's lives, that makes a difference here and into eternity . Through her story we can see that we are never alone. Thank you, Diana, for having the courage to share your story."

David Dietrich

"The book by Diana Jimison, '*YOU CAN MAKE IT! A Story of Redemption, Grace and Perseverance*', will encourage anyone! It is exactly as the title states, a true story of a person with whom most can identify. As all of us encounter blessings and struggles in our minds, families, friends, vocation and faith, this testimony reveals the way through it all successfully – a dynamic faith in Jesus Christ! Those presently struggling through such issues can receive great strength, motivation and hope from Diana's experiences. This message reveals the truth of God's Word that Satan has come *'to kill, steal and destroy.'*; but Jesus came that He can be *'the way, truth and the life.'* Diana discovered that, through Jesus Christ, *YOU CAN MAKE IT!*"

- Rev. Bobby Gilley

"God uses specific people in certain times to fulfill his plan & will for a person's life. His grace & mercy are always there; he just needs people willing to obey him. I could say a lot more about the miraculous miracles that took place in your life & what God did in your early years of Christianity. You are a miracle of God. You & your family are very special to us."

Love & prayers,
John & Judy Miles

"The enemy tries to destroy believers by convincing us we are alone and that no one understands. Your words remind me that our battle is not unique and that we all face struggles in life. Your faith in Christ and commitment to His purpose is evident in your words. Thank you for proclaiming the love of Jesus and sharing your testimony with the world. I love you, friend!"

-Dr. Angela Elliott Melson

ABOUT THE AUTHOR

Diana Jimison is a wife, mother, and registered nurse. Diana has worked in several healthcare venues, from the hospital setting to home-health and outpatient practices with a focus in case management for the previous 5 years. Her ultimate passion is for all to have a personal relationship and encounter with Jesus Christ. Diana and her husband have one daughter and reside in Hickory, NC.

INTRODUCTION

This book serves a twofold purpose; to provide encouragement for those who have faced and those who will face difficult times and to glorify Jesus, who has kept my mind, and has given me strength to overcome the pain without being addicted to medication or losing my mind through the struggles. I live because He lives. There are many examples of my failures and successes that may help you along your journey. I prefer to learn from other people's mistakes.

I am certain as you read this book that you may identify with certain circumstances. You may even find yourself crying as you relate to one or more of the events. It's ok. God tells us in His Word, "You keep track of all my sorrows. You have collected all my tears in your bottle. You have recorded each one in your book" (Psalm 56:8, NIV).

I have been compelled to share my testimony for years, but phrases like, "Who do you think you are?" or "No one wants to hear what you have to say" kept running through my head, along with severe physical issues that deterred me for quite some time. The question I had to ask myself is which voice will I choose to listen to? I am trusting as I move forward in obedience that many lives will be positively affected for His glory.

I believe the Lord spoke to my heart a few years ago when Pat Schatzline was at our church for "Surge the City". I had taken a friend to church with me that night and I heard in my spirit, "I want you to write a book." My heart started beating fast. After pondering on the idea and explaining it away, I ignored the thought and put it on the shelf. Life and fatigue have also greatly interfered. I had attempted on several occasions but computers would crash causing me to lose my work several times, and I had not saved the work to a hard drive. With each attempt, it just got tougher for me to get past certain things along with the overwhelming question, "How can God use you?" that plagued my mind.

I feel strongly that I have not walked in obedience. I had given my testimony in church once, and was told by several I should write a book. There were very few dry eyes that night, and I felt such a relief. I still feel very strong that sharing my story is what I am supposed to do. I am going to trust that this will encourage every day normal people like you and I to not give up, to run the race with endurance and to prayerfully be used to change lives along this journey.

I was recently reminded of Jonah and how he tried to run from what God had called him to do and how God brought storms in his life until he returned with a heart of obedience.

In my earlier years as a Christian, I could listen to messages while I worked. I used to love to hear testimonies on the program "Focus on the Family." They would inspire me to not give up and to serve God with passion. One of my favorite scriptures is found in the Book of Revelations 12:11: "They overcame him by the blood of the Lamb and by the word of their testimony." Overcame who? The accuser of our souls.

My prayer is that you will be encouraged and gain strength in your trials. God never promised life would be easy. He promised He would be with us through the storms of our lives. Let us, as a body of believers, unite, stand together, and be strong for truly the signs are here and the final days are upon us. Whether you believe that or not, I think we all can agree we are only here for a short time as scriptures tell us our life is but a vapor that vanishes away (James 4:14).

I believe each and every one of us have been given purpose and were created for greatness. The enemy will never tell you to complete a task that will help build up and edify. He wants to paralyze us, keep us busy with things that do not have eternal value. Whatever God has called us to do, let's do with excellency. We need to be the light in our workplace, to be the example in our homes, and to show the love of God to the hurting. We must hear their cries and move forward with purpose.

Due to the nature of the tragedies in my life and the frequency of those tragedies, I have not been able to nurture or keep very many close relationships. I thank God for those He has brought in my life that have impacted me tremendously and have helped me be a better me. You will hear more about each of these individuals in the book: The McDaniel family, Pastor John C. Miles and Judy Miles, David Dietrich, Sam and Sandy Crowe, The Chronister family, Mr. Tracy Robinson, Mike and Chelsea Nash, Sara Seitz, Melanie Fox, and my precious Aunt Barbara. We all have those special somebody's who speak into our lives, who believe in us, who help us during hard times, and those who don't give up on us.

I am also thankful for the ministers of the gospel that have spoken words of life through their messages over the years: John C. Miles, Bobby Gilley, Same Crowe, Mark Ivey, Pat Schatzline, Joe Phillips, Karen Wheaton, Perry Stone, Fred Stone, Jentezen Franklin, Paula White, Joyce Meyers, Beth Moore, Dwight Thompson, Rod Parsley, T.L. Lowry, E.L. Terry, Reinhard Bonke, Greg Laurie, James McDonald, Chip Ingram, the Reverend Billy Graham, and most recently Steven Furtick, and Jeremiah Johnson, along with many others. I am so thankful for Christian television and Christian radio stations, as I am strengthened by them and appreciate those who have worked so hard to make it happen.

My prayer is that lives will be changed, that you will understand your purpose, know your assignment, and know that God is the source of your strength. He will sustain you and help you overcome no matter what you are facing. I pray healings will take place in your body, mind and spirit. I pray relationships will be restored, financial burdens will be lifted, and most of all that we will be ready and walking in obedience when the day comes that He calls us home in the mighty name of Jesus.

I'm pretty sure there will be those who will judge me, but that's ok. I judge myself according to the scriptures and am easily convicted by the Spirit of God and trust that He is the Protector of my soul. It is never my desire to offend anyone, and I am truly sorry for those I have hurt along the way. What I do know is no one is perfect. We all have issues that need to be brought before the cross, and the greatest gift we could give one another is to lift each other up in prayer. I am so thankful we serve a gracious, merciful and just God.

I am not a theologian, nor a Bible scholar. I don't have some deep revelation to share other than the greatest revelation given to any man, boy, woman or girl: JESUS CHRIST IS THE SON OF GOD. I am just an ordinary individual with a story that conveys God's miraculous grace and infinite love. I pray you will be able to take something from it, and that you will literally feel God's arms around you; especially if you are facing difficulties and uncertainties.

Nationally, we are facing many things as we approach the 2016 election. Judgment begins first in God's house (1 Peter 4:17). The wheat will be separated from the tares and God's Remnant will arise. (Matthew 3:12). We need to get serious about what we believe and walk it out. Let's pray for one another.

I want to clarify that my writings in no way are meant to disrespect my parents. I love them so much. My parents were decent people for those who didn't go to church. I would say "good" but Jesus rebuked someone for calling Him good.

"There is none good but my Father in heaven" (Luke 18:19). My recollections are as close as they can be from what I can remember. There are some incidences in my life, I choose to leave out because they are too shameful for me to speak of; others I just choose at this time not to disclose. I have tried to protect individuals, as my main goal is to convey how God rescued me and has kept me through my experiences. I promise if you hang on and get through the details you will see just how amazing our God is, and how He can pull anyone from the trenches of hell and literally transform their life to reflect His goodness and His love.

I have permission from my husband to be transparent. I won't disclose some of our struggles. We don't have the perfect marriage. We have had really difficult times, but both of us are committed to making it work. As long as we both keep God a priority in our lives, all things are possible. Whether he does or not...my eyes are on the King. The divorce rate is rising even more so in evangelical homes, and we must be aware the enemy of our soul knows that if he can destroy the family then it will have a negative impact on the body of Christ. We cannot let that slew foot win.

CHAPTER ONE

"Three little monkeys jumping on the bed, one fell off and bumped its head. Momma called the doctor and the doctor said, 'No more monkeys jumping on the bed'"[1].

This is what I envision as I think about me and my brothers as we jumped on the bed together, happy with no cares in the world. Our parents were really young when they married. Mom was 15 and

---

[1] Song lyrics from "Five Little Monkeys", an English language folk song (writer unknown)

daddy was 17. Momma had all three of us kiddos by the time she was 18. Life wasn't easy for them. They didn't have much support. Daddy had been drafted to serve in the army but due to my mother having such a difficult time, he was granted an honorable discharge.

We lived in a mobile home park when we were smaller. This is where my baby brother, Robert got hurt on his little bike, sustained a deep cut on his chin and was rushed to the emergency room for stitches. I can still see his blonde hair glistening as the sunbeams strike against each strand and him crying. We later moved to a little house in Hickory and stayed there until I finished the 4th grade. This house has since been torn down for stores.

A few things I remembered while being at this house. I stepped on a board with a nail and it went into my foot. I fell out of my daddy's car while he was pulling out of a store on HWY 127. Seat belt laws weren't as strict back then. One of our dogs we loved was run over by a car. My cousin, Theresa Osment, stayed with us quite a bit during this time. Momma loved her dearly. We went to Jenkins Elementary. I had repeated nightmares of apes chasing me and Robert.

Overall, we seemed to be a pretty happy family. Momma took pictures of us and you could see how close we were during this time in our lives.

I love my momma more than words can express. I always felt something terrible happened to her in the past. She was a very private individual who didn't discuss her childhood which led me to believe it was painful. Her daddy passed away when she was 15, which was probably the reason why she married so young and felt like she needed my daddy. My momma was a tough cookie, but I would find her crying behind closed doors when no one was looking. She was not a socialite and didn't really have friends, but she would give anyone the shirt off of her back. Daddy was her best friend. Looking back, she seemed to be such a lonely person and this saddens me. She dealt with situations the best she knew how. She was pretty much the disciplinarian. She tried different ways to discipline us, some more harsh than others. While in the 3rd grade there was a period of time that all 3 of us would get a whippin' after we got home from the paper route. It was just expected and yes, I dreaded going home during that time. There were other times that we were made to stay in our room and write sentences the entire day, until it felt like my hands were going to fall off. We were pretty good kids, knowing never to cross the line to "smart-off" to momma, but I would take chances with my daddy.

Daddy was a character, totally opposite from my momma. He never met a stranger. He didn't talk about his upbringing either. What I know of his past, I learned from my aunt. You would never know he had been raised in such poor conditions because of his personality. He pretty much stayed on the streets from around the age of 11. He was a gentle man but he also had a temper. He was a handsome fellow who worked at a gas station in his teens. It has been said by those who knew him that "he was a pistol."

Both my parents had quit school but went back later to get their General Education Diploma. My daddy was intelligent. He could have had a career to where he didn't have to do such hard manual labor if someone had just believed in him. One of my fondest memories was when daddy would get ready on Saturdays and take us to the store and buy us a candy bar and a Coke. He would just hang out talking to whomever came in.

My parents worked hard to provide a roof over our head. There wasn't much left for extras. School shopping was minimal, maybe 2 outfits a year if we were fortunate. I would see momma scrounge for coins to buy herself something like a little pickled sausage. I never saw her eat much. Daddy ended up working 3 jobs to pay the bills and take care of us. After we moved we didn't get to see him often; and when I did see him he would be at the kitchen table figuring out the bills...worrying. He was a work horse and took pride in taking care of his family. My mom wasn't high maintenance. She wore t-shirts and blue jeans. She would wear soles out of the bottom of her shoes and holes in her jeans before she would buy another pair.

My parents struggled with child care with 3 children. Daddy's parents would watch us sometimes. My grandmother would pinch and scratch me and throw me outside while my brothers were kept inside. When momma and daddy found out about this, they stopped taking us over there to stay.

I was the middle child and was usually asked questions like, "Hey aren't you Ricky's sister?" or "Aren't you Robert's sister?" Robert was the baby and the clown of the family. Ricky was the one who liked to tear things up and would get in so much trouble if he didn't get it put back together. This would come in handy for him when he got older. I was the smartest of the three, which really depended on who looked at it. My daddy always said I may have book smarts but not enough sense to come in out of the rain. His way of thinking was if he told me I couldn't do something then it would make me want to try harder.

Our parents raised us the best they knew how and with what little they were given during their childhood. We were called names like fat---. Whoever said words don't hurt has never been the recipient of painful words. My brothers were told they would not amount to anything. I always wanted to be close to my mom, to hear her tell me she loved me, to go places with her and do things. I tried to earn my parents love, mostly my mom's. I felt like I was a good girl and honestly my brothers were pretty good too. I stayed out of trouble and always made the honor roll. I tried to help my mom and enjoyed helping her, but she was pretty adamant about doing most things herself. I wanted to learn how to cook, but we weren't allowed in the kitchen. She had to grow up way too fast and didn't really have the chance to enjoy being a teenager herself. My brothers yearned for our father's love. He was pretty hard on both of them. I think having 3 children and the stress of all the bills was just overwhelming for the both of them. They didn't abuse the government like we see people doing today. They worked hard to try to make it on their own and were too prideful to ask for help and they didn't have family that were in a financial position to help them along the way.

I know how detrimental negative words can be especially for someone who does not know their identity in Christ. Proverbs 18:21 tells us that life and death are in the power of the tongue. You can literally break a child's spirit with words. If you do these things, please stop! Your children are not mistakes. They are gifts, and we are responsible for each and every word we speak if they have not been forgiven. I find myself having to counteract and cancel out words that even my husband and I have spoken at times. I let something come out of my mouth once towards my precious daughter. I purposed in my heart I would not say hurtful things to her. I didn't want to have this quality that my parents possessed whether intentional or unintentional. It takes discipline and determination to rise above these behaviors. I will never forget the look on her face when the words just flowed out of my mouth, "Can't you do anything right?" I don't even know where that came from, but I'll never be able to get those words back.   I apologized repeatedly as tears ran down my face. I could not believe I said those things out of frustration. In our home, it is certainly known that we aren't perfect. We fall short and each of us must practice forgiveness and trust God to heal the wounds. Have you been there or am I the only one to crush their daughter's spirit? This is one of those rotten examples you can learn from and not bring offense to your precious children. Stress can cause a person to act in very unbecoming ways.

CHAPTER TWO

I was about 6 or 7 when we moved into our new home. Looking back, I could see a shifting and decline in the joy we shared as a family. I remember momma saying later she wished we had never moved. Daddy had gotten a job delivering newspapers. We had to help them in the middle of the night. Rain, sleet or snow, we had to go. They had a little Toyota and I can remember the three of us crawling in the floorboard to try to stay warm and that is where we would fall asleep in that little car. We took turns as we got older getting up and going on the routes; how I dreaded Sundays. Those papers were so big and my hands would hurt terribly. Daddy had a really huge route and soon both my parents would end up with two more routes for a total of three paper routes. If you don't tip the paper guy or gal, let me encourage you to do that! Until you've actually delivered newspapers you would never know how hard it is. My daddy would get so tickled when he would get tips for Christmas. Although I hated it with a passion, it was my parent's livelihood. God has people in every type of business that will show His love and speak life into others.

My brothers and I were pretty close. Don't get me wrong! Robert and I could have some drag out fights, but I loved my brothers and didn't put up with anyone mistreating them. I was jealous because they got to do things that I couldn't do. Ricky got a bike for Christmas one year, but he got hurt so that ruined the chance for me or Robert to have a bike. I never learned to ride a bike, to swim or to skate while growing up. My brothers and I weren't allowed to talk on the phone. What would this generation do? I guess you can't miss something you never really had? I enjoyed sports during PE. I was pretty fast and competitive in elementary school before I entered the 7th grade. My mom grounded us for the entire summer prior which was the beginning of our problems with weight.

I gained almost 50 pounds that year. This was traumatic for me.

Being overweight in middle school was difficult. I was so wrapped up in wanting to be "normal" that it became an addiction to me. I had always wanted to play sports, but was never allowed. I didn't ask because we just knew we weren't allowed to do those things. We had never gone to a football or basketball game. We didn't know what that lifestyle was. I remember wanting so badly to be a part of clubs. Ricky did get to join band but it was too much for my mom to keep up with and it was a hassle she wasn't willing to continue. After school, we went straight to pick up papers to deliver. It took hours to get the route done, and we would get home with black ink all over us. We were only allowed to take two baths a week: on Sunday and Wednesday. I'm not really sure why, but as teenagers, this wasn't in our favor. I remembered how I wanted to wash my hair so badly that I would sneak and wash it in the mornings when momma was asleep. She caught me once. I didn't like being scolded by her. I wanted to please her.

I wanted to wear makeup and just fit in. I stole some makeup from a store that my mom would stop by frequently after the paper route. She would have me run in to get a few things. Management caught me and told me not to come back in the store. How could I tell my mom? I didn't. I just risked it each time I would have to go back in, with my heart beating so fast.   I can remember stealing 2 other times during my childhood. Once was in elementary school. I stole a piece of chewing gum. The teacher who caught me put the fear of God in me. I hadn't heard much about God except when His name was taken in vain. The entire class was punished, because I had not come forth. Another time I recall someone using the speaker system and calling security to an aisle. I was in a store with my dad and stole some shoes I wanted to get for my momma. I ran out to the car without being caught. That scared me enough to not want to do that again. The truth was I had already broken several of the commandments...do not lie, do not steal. I heard someone dear once say, "You don't have to teach a child not to sin because we are born into sin. You have to teach them how to obey." Romans 3: 23 tells us that "...all have sinned."

When I started the 7th grade, I saw a familiar face from where we delivered newspapers. Her name was Shannon and we soon became friends. I was around 12 when my mom finally allowed me to spend the night with Shannon. I got to go to church with them a few times. Larry, her dad, taught Sunday school and the first message I ever remember hearing was on Nebuchadnezzar. I just remember that name specifically. Ole Nebby. Crazy huh? There was something different about this family. I longed to have the love that they shared. I had been to church with my aunt

Kay when I was really young, and my brothers and I had briefly ridden a church bus. I recall winning a cake one Sunday at church. We stopped going for some reason. We were so young; I cannot remember any other details.

Things began to change for the worse as I got older. I stayed the summer with my grandmother who had broken her leg. I felt like I was an outsider, as if I didn't belong there and it seemed that I was getting farther away from having a close relationship with my mom. I started my cycle at the age of 9. I was so scared that I had done something wrong. I was clueless, so I had gone to my daddy out of fear. Momma got so mad at me for not going to her. This was the beginning of noticeable change in our relationship. Things kept adding fuel to an already volatile relationship. I had also been sexually abused by a close friend of the family, who had fondled me in private places for years by the time I became a teenager. I had grown to have strong feelings for him and longed for his attention. I didn't know how to emotionally handle this. I had carried this with me since I was 6 or 7. I had accidentally mentioned something to someone at school. Next thing I knew, DSS came to my home. My parents nailed the windows shut and made me feel like it was all my fault. They made me feel that I was an embarrassment to them. This may not have been how they felt, but it was how I remember feeling. I had not only lost their trust, but also lost that false sense of love when I was around him.

PERSONAL INSIGHT

If you are in a situation like this where you feel that no one loves you or cares for you, I encourage you not to look for anyone's approval or for a false sense of security found in the arms of someone who doesn't care about you. I want to point you to the One who can satisfy every longing in your soul: Jesus. You are so important to Him. Ladies, you are a princess in His eyes.

Gentlemen, you are called Sons of the Most High King. He can send the right people in your path at the right time when you need it most and, until that happens, I promise you, He is all you need. I think of Ruth and how God ordered her steps out of Moab because she wanted to follow Naomi back to her homeland and serve her God. It looked gloomy for Naomi. She could not offer Ruth a husband because she had lost her husband and both her sons. Ruth did not care. Her mind was made up and nothing could change it. Ruth gleaned the fields and while doing so found favor in the eyes of Boaz who would soon become her husband. Ladies don't settle for just anyone. Run passionately after God and do not settle for anyone who is not doing the same. This will save you a lot of heartache and pain. Take time to read Ruth if you have never done so.

Things were getting ready to drastically change and for the worse. I convinced my parents to allow me to get a job. This is where I became exposed to different lifestyles: teenagers with more freedom and high school dropouts. My behavior began to change. Up to this point, I had been an A-B honor roll student. I didn't use foul language except for once when my brothers and I were young and took turns trying to recite all the bad words we knew. Oh, my!! I was in AG classes, so I didn't get picked on like my brothers did. Music was my outlet but I listened to toxic music: "I'm on the Highway to Hell." I filled my soul with garbage that I understand would one day directly influence me. Did you know that Satan, hence Lucifer, was the music director in Heaven? In my study, the Bible doesn't specifically say this, but I think it is safe to conclude he was from the scriptures Isaiah 14: 11-14 and Ezekiel 28: 13-16. Do you know that for everything God has created Satan has a counterfeit version and will use as a destructive device in our lives if we allow him to?

My daddy and I would get into heated arguments. I was already abusing my body by binging and purging. I had picked up some other things along the way that I had become exposed to through ungodly literature. When I would get so angry and hurt I would just literally beat myself with my own fists in fits of rage. If I had known about cutting I would most likely have implemented this destructive behavior. I obtained some speed from someone at work because I had heard it would help me lose weight. I got in a fight with my daddy on the paper route one night. I can't remember what it was about, but I do remember taking hit after hit of those pink hearts. I was an emotionally disturbed teenager. I am so thankful I didn't die that night. Let's just say I felt like I was going to. "Are you taking anything?" asked daddy. While crying, I told him no. It was a horrible night. I had always done my own work. I would help my brother, Ricky, with his homework but that night I could not do my own from throwing up the entire night.

I had a book report due. I remember the compassion my momma had towards me. She read the book for me and did the report, another dishonest action on my part.

PERSONAL INSIGHT

If you are reading this and you are actively causing harm to your body, please seek godly counsel from those who will not judge you. I promise God has an army of individuals who will wrap their arms around you and not judge you. I found relief in anointed services where the presence of God was so strong that it broke the power this had over my life. Bodily harm is an attack of the enemy to make you think there is no hope and there is relief when you cut or do drugs, binge or purge. No, this is a lie! This is not healthy. Our body is the temple where God dwells. We cannot walk in God's full purpose for our life while partaking in these things. The devil knows God's word. He knows the scripture that says if we destroy the temple of God's spirit then He will destroy us (1

Corinthians 3:17). This is what he wants and as believers we must shed light on this. If you don't have the willpower to just stop these behaviors, find yourself in a God-fearing church that allows His Spirit to move and I promise you, God will deliver you from these destructive behaviors! Don't forget to seek godly counsel.

God, I pray for each and every one who may be reading this who feels their answer lies in these destructive behaviors. I ask that you would break the chains that have them bound. I pray against this wicked scheme of the enemy. Deliver each one in Jesus name.

CHAPTER THREE

I reached the point where I had become disrespectful to my parents. Full blown rebellion had set into my heart. One incident I remember momma just taking a belt and slinging it at me because she was so mad. Some things had taken place with a few individuals where I worked. Next thing I knew, I had packed a large black garbage bag full of my things and had someone pick me up in the middle of the night at the age of 15. I went to live with my momma's sister and then moved on to another aunt whose husband was obnoxious. He tried to rule me with an iron fist to keep me from doing my own thing. I had gotten involved in pure ungodliness and an immoral lifestyle. Nevertheless, I attempted to stay in school. I was writing awful letters to guys, going back and forth with vulgarity. I continued with binging and purging, through taking laxatives. I had an episode where I dropped all my books one day when sharp pains literally paralyzed me. The school called my mom who came and got me. She took me to the hospital but she told me to never call her again. The excessive use of laxatives was causing me problems.

When my uncle realized he could not rule me, he took all of my belongings and threw them in front of the Kroger grocery store where I worked. This was the beginning of my homelessness. I would hitch hike and stay in cheap hotels. I would walk through the area we called "the hill" in the middle of the night, knowing now that it was only by God's amazing grace I was not killed. I was fearless, not having a care in the world. I had no idea if I would have died during these years, I would have gone to hell.

My mother took me to court when I was 16 years old to have me emancipated. She didn't want to be held accountable for things I was doing or may do. It amazed me how I convinced a judge that I had enough sense to take care of myself, working at

Kroger's making a huge $4.10 an hour. The inevitable finally happened and I was forced to quit school. I went from an A/B honor student to a high school dropout. Who you hang around, you become? Out of all the things I had done, I found out later that quitting school is what hurt my daddy the most. Even though he would speak negative things to me, he always thought I was going to be the first one to go to college in our family.

NORTH CAROLINA   IN THE GENERAL COURT OF JUSTICE
                                  DISTRICT COURT DIVISION
CATAWBA COUNTY   JUVENILE DEPARTMENT
                                  HICKORY, NORTH CAROLINA
                                  FILE NO. _____

DIANA RENAE REINHARDT,   )
        Petitioner,   )
    vs.   )   PETITION FOR
)   EMANCIPATION
RICHARD DEAN REINHARDT   )
and KATHY M. REINHARDT   )
        Respondents.   )

        The Petitioner, Diana Renae Reinhardt, respectfully
shows unto the Court as follows:

        1.   The Petitioner, Diana Renae Reinhardt, was born
_____, in Catawba County, North Carolina;

        2.   The Petitioner has been a resident of Catawba
County, North Carolina, for at least six months next
preceding the filing of this Petition;

        3.   A certified copy of the Petitioner's birth
certificate is attached to this Petition as Exhibit 1 and
incorporated herein by reference;

        4.   The Petitioner's parents are Richard Dean
Reinhardt and Kathy Sue Reinhardt, whose address is _____
_____;

        5.   The Petitioner's address is _____
Hickory, North Carolina 28601 and she has lived at that
address since April 13, 1989;

        6.   The Petitioner is requesting emancipation for the
following reasons:

        a.   The Petitioner has been living out of the family
residence for a number of months, attending school and
supporting herself and finds that this arrangement is the
one most suitable to her;

        b.   The Petitioner has had disagreements with her
parents when she was living in the family home;

        c.   The Petitioner has shown an ability to support
herself and make decisions for herself while living on her
own and she wishes to continue in this manner;

I found people to stay with here and there. I think about all the situations I found myself in where I could have been killed. I quit Kroger's and got a job at a fast food restaurant. I worked there for several years, working my way up to the position of assistant manager all while going deeper and deeper into sin and bondage. One of the guys I had feelings for from my first job experience asked me one night in a hotel, "Do you know you will go to hell for what you are doing?" I hadn't thought much about heaven or hell. None really. I had not heard much about either. I was participating in an ungodly, immoral lifestyle, sexual immorality and at one point interested in the occult. I was interested in joining the occult but the ritual at that time was sacrificing a finger which was a little extreme for me. Little did I know I was already one of Satan's servants.

Some time had passed when I decided to go see momma and daddy. I remember seeing my baby brother and him telling me he missed me. He had grown into a handsome young man. Momma was still in bed that morning, but daddy was awake and told me I needed to leave before she woke up. I looked around and saw places on the walls that were not completely saturated with nicotine, and realized my pictures were gone; only my brothers' remained. All the pain I had buried was brought instantly back to the surface. I didn't know how I could hide or run from it. When I think about all the pain that I caused my parents and what they had lost, it breaks my heart. I can imagine their sleepless nights and the pangs in my momma's stomach that only a mother of a wayward child can know. I can see how she probably had to remove the pictures to be able to deal with losing her daughter. Things hadn't turned out exactly how she had planned or hoped.

Years passed and I can't remember how much time had lapsed before I reconnected with my friend Shannon and her family. It had to be sometime in 1990, because they had invited me to a Carman concert that December. I had never been to anything like that before. I had been to one concert before: Janet Jackson. There was a huge difference between the two. There were so many people everywhere, singing and raising their hands. The atmosphere was different. It was a Divine set-up. The New Year came and it was 1991. I was 18 years old and was heading into a pit of depression, thinking about how I was supposed to be graduating and how I was supposed to be a doctor. After spending time evaluating the mess I had made of my life, I just wanted to end it.

I can't recall how I re-entered my parents' lives, but at some point, this had transpired, because I had my own apartment at 17 and they were the ones who gave me the $400 deposit I needed. I was there in February, alone and meditating how I could just end it all right there in my bathroom. As I was contemplating, I began to weep as something unusual began to stir in me. I felt an overwhelming presence in the room. I had no idea what was getting ready to happen. As I mentioned before I had only gone to church a few times. I couldn't tell you about Moses, Noah or Zacchaeus who climbed up in a tree, but somehow I knew enough to pray a prayer that would set me free from the bondages of sin and shame. I told God that night that if He would forgive me of my sins, I would serve him the rest of my life.

For the first time in my life, I felt like I only weighed one pound. It literally felt like a mountain had been removed from my shoulders. I was in a tough situation though. My sins had me tangled in a vicious web, and I didn't know how I was going to get out of it.

How many of you can testify that God can untangle the mess we create and as we look back to see how we survived all we can say is to God be all of the glory? How many of you also know when you are "born again", "saved", or "REDEEMED" that you can't keep quiet? In Matthew 8:4, after Jesus healed the leper he said, "Go and tell no one but go first to the priest and let them examine you. This will be a public testimony that you have been healed." Can you imagine what this man did after he went to the priest? I can see him running immediately back to his family to reunite and share how Jesus, the Son of God was willing to heal his body. When you get cleaned up on the inside, it's impossible not to tell everyone you know what Jesus has done for you. Not only will you declare this with your mouth, but there will be a transformation in your talk and walk. It is a process but the change will be evident. 2 Corinthians 5: 17 (NIV) states, "Therefore, if anyone is in Christ, the new creation has come: The old has gone, the new is here!"

I was so excited about what had happened that I went first to tell my parents. My daddy said, "You won't last two weeks." My momma told me, "Don't talk to me about God, or you won't be welcomed in my home." I guess I didn't know what I expected them to say, but I knew something had happened that I couldn't explain. I didn't fully understand how it would literally change the direction of my life. I wanted to learn all I could about this man called Jesus.

PERSONAL INSIGHT

Beware of the "negative Nellies" in your life. The devil will try to discourage you in your new-found faith, the call on your life, or specific instructions that God has given you to complete. Just like he has tried to do with the writing of this book. In John 10:10 (NIV), the Bible says that "the thief comes only to steal and kill and destroy; BUT I have come that they may have life, and have it to the full."

Just because I had made a decision that literally saved my life that night, and ultimately would make my life better didn't mean it was going to happen overnight and the devil's passé wasn't going to make it easy on me either. The Bible tells us "the thief comes to steal, kill and destroy" (John 10:10) and he was using every tactic to get me to fail, to sin, and to make me believe I wasn't worthy of God's love. I am so thankful that someone loved me enough like Cathy, Shannon's mom, to encourage me in God's Word, and not to give up. She would say "Diana, the Word of God says if we confess your sins He is faithful and just to forgive us of our sin" (1 John 1: 9, NIV). She did not beat me into the ground or judge me. She loved me all the way to the Cross. God had put forgiveness in my heart for my parents and a new-found love for my family. I didn't blame them for my childhood. They had done the best they could with that they had been given. They did not have any Godly influences in their lives and I realized they loved me and my brothers the best way they knew how.

CHAPTER FOUR

Two months had passed, and I had been attending church with Shannon's family. They attended a revival at the Longview Church of God and had invited me. Here I would meet more of the McDaniel family (Larry's daughter, Aundria, and her babies, Jenica and Krisina) who have a special place in my heart today. Things would come full circle in 2011 when Kris would be the one to invite me to the church I am at today. I've seen those girls grow up and have cried many tears over them and their lives. They are very special to me.

There was something different in the way this church worshipped. It was lively while everyone clapped their hands to the worship music, singing with joy. The evangelist, Bobby Gilley, was preaching and it wasn't by chance that I was there that week. God had orchestrated my footsteps because He knew I needed the anointing to break the yokes of bondage over my life from such immorality. It was during this revival on April 16, 1991 that I received the baptism of the Holy Ghost and began to speak in other tongues as the Spirit gave the utterance, two months after giving my heart to Jesus in my bathroom. Actually, I had stammering lips and didn't speak in words that night. I was in my apartment one day spending time in the Word and in prayer, and I began to speak in a beautiful language. This was when I was single and could just spend hours in prayer. I knew something supernatural had taken place in my life and it proved to me that God's Word is absolutely true. Jesus said, "If I go not away, the Comforter [or some versions say Helper] will not come. But when I go away, I will send Him to you" (John 16:7). This experience is not just so one can say they speak in tongues, but so you can be endued with power from on high. Power to say no to sin, to boldly proclaim God's Word and speak His truth into lives lost without Him.

I had not been inundated with religion and man's theologies, so I was prepared to receive all that God had for me during this revival. He changed my heart and the way I talked. I used the filthiest language. My parents didn't use the "f-word". I was led to believe that was the worst word you could say, but taking God's name in vain is by far the worse. Exodus 20:7 (NIV) states, "You shall not misuse the name of the LORD your God, for the LORD will not hold anyone guiltless who misuses his name." It grieves the Holy Spirit, and I am careful to not speak His name unless it is used reverently. His name is Holy. Neither, do I promote Hollywood propaganda that takes His name in vain, and I pray I will always hold true to this.

PERSONAL INSIGHT

Do you hunger for more of God in your walk? Have you been taught that one shouldn't speak in tongues without an interpreter or that it is of the devil? This is exactly what the devil wants you to believe.

The gift of the Holy Ghost is an experience that empowers you. When you don't know what to pray, you can pray in the Holy Spirit which bypasses the natural language barrier and goes straight to our Father. When I don't know how to pray about a situation I will pray in the Spirit and sometimes with groanings. Romans 8: 26 (NIV) says, "In the same way, the Spirit helps us in our weakness. We do not know what we ought to pray for, but the Spirit himself intercedes for us through wordless groans."

According to an article published in the New York Times, "Contrary to what may be a common perception, studies suggest that people who speak in tongues rarely suffer from mental problems. A recent study of nearly 1,000 evangelical Christians in England found that those who engaged in the practice were more emotionally stable than those who did not."[2] **Keep this in mind as you read the accounts of my life.**

I convinced my brother to go to church with me one night that week. The Holy Spirit moved in such a powerful way. Robert got up and walked out of the church during the altar service. He would later ask me, "Sissy, did you talk to that preacher about me?" I told him, "No, but God did." I later allowed my brother to move in with me. He had become addicted to alcohol. Someone in our neighborhood had given it to him after I had left home when he was around 14 years old. I helped him get a job working with me. He had met a sweet girl whose parents had forbidden her to date him. Robert was such a handsome, sweet-natured boy except when he was drinking. He could not get over her. He tried to find peace in a bottle. I applaud this young lady's parents, but it was not easy seeing

[2] Carey, B. (2006, November 7). *A Neuroscientific Look at Speaking in Tongues.* Retrieved from http://www.nytimes.com/2006/11/07/health/07brain.html

my brother heartbroken. He had no place to go, so I let him move in with me and naturally I had to set some boundaries. With my new-found relationship with Jesus, I didn't want to enable or encourage something that Jesus spoke against. Proverbs 20:1 (NIV) states, "Wine is a mocker and beer a brawler, whoever is led astray by them is not wise."

I would show Robert lots of love and compassion. He would call me in the middle of the night to come get him on the side of the road, in jail or at parties, almost getting me mauled over by those he would make angry. He called me once at work and was in a frantic, "Sissy come get me, they are after me; there's a riot, sissy." My heart racing, I got to him in time but drove away in fear for our lives, looking back to see if we were being followed.

One night I came home and found alcohol in my apartment and I lost it. Being a new Christian, there were things I struggled with, and even now, 26 years later, I struggle with different things. I was willing to help him all that I could, but I wasn't willing to provide a place where he could stay and drink. I yelled at him, said some words that broke the heart of God and cried myself to sleep. It wasn't easy for me to let him go, and I struggled with it for some time. I have always wanted to protect my brothers. He left and I didn't hear from him for some time. I received a handwritten letter from a gentleman that read: "I have just recently given Robert a job out of town in Atlanta, Georgia. The job is just a summer job. At any time, he feels like he wants to come back I will bring him or put him on a bus. So please don't worry about him. He will have no time to get into trouble. We work 6 days a week and 10 hours a day. I am hiring him as a helper at $6 an hour doing vinyl siding construction." Robert adds to the letter, "Sissy will you keep my stuff here until I can get a chance to come by and get it? I'll probably be back in about 2 months and take care of it then.

Will you call the store and have them mail my check, and I'll take care of that when I come back. I'm sorry for all the trouble I caused here, ok? I love you Bye. Love Robert." This was so considerate of this young man to send me a letter. You can tell by his words that Robert knew I loved him and that I was worried about him. I cry every time I come across the letter because it brings back floods of memories.

CHAPTER FIVE

During this time I continued praying, seeking God, reading His Word and going to church...the most important actions of any believer during every stage of their walk with God. I was 18 years old trying to find a place to fit in. It didn't take me long to realize that I needed to be in the young adult class because of my previous lifestyle and all I had done causing me to grow up more quickly than your average teenager. I'll never forget what my Sunday school teacher, David Dietrich, told me one night at the altar. "Don't take my word or anyone else's word as the gospel. Study God's Word and ask Him to reveal His truth to you and He will." That became one of the many solid building blocks of my faith. I continued to grow under the ministry of Reverend John C. Miles. He became a spiritual father to me. He and his wife, Judy, loved me. They helped me and gave me instruction that has enabled me to be the person I am today. They taught me what integrity looked like, and I will forever be grateful to God for placing them in my life. It's harder to find this type of discipleship in the bigger churches today. That's why it is imperative to participate in small groups and connect with those who will speak into your life. You must have a teachable spirit and not get angry when someone attempts to direct you in love. This is part of the growing process.

A year and half passed and several new folks came to the church, one of those being Mr. James Jimison. I was not interested in a relationship. I was in love with Jesus, trying to bring as many as I could to Him. James had not been a Christian for long (about 3 months) when he came to Longview. He had received the Baptism of the Holy Ghost and was on fire for God. He and his friends came and sat on the front row of the church. You know something has happened if you're brave enough to sit on the front row!! Several of his friends and my friends would go to revivals together and have prayer meetings and Bible studies. It was odd how things came about because my friend, whom I had the privilege to greatly influence her decision for Christ, was interested in Mr. Jimison. I highly encouraged her to be interested in him. For whatever reason, James liked me, although my friend was much prettier and could sing like an angel.

After dating less than one month, James and I were married. Let me be clear: I do not advise this for anyone unless you have absolutely heard from heaven. If it were not for God's grace, and our desire to serve God, we would not be able to say that we celebrated our 23rd Anniversary in May of 2016. It has not been easy. Pastor Miles asked me, "Diana are you sure you want to do this?" I think he knew he would not be able to convince me otherwise.

The church was so good to us. I didn't know anything about weddings. So many pitched in to make our wedding day memorable. Jeff Kilby took pictures, the ladies (including Cindy Dietrich and Brenda Lippard) provided a reception for us. Every flower and bouquet was provided and the dress was borrowed from my friend Shannon. We didn't have any money and I had never anticipated having a real wedding but the love that the church showed us was more than we deserved. Isn't that just like God? My daddy walked me down the aisle. We had a tape playing "The Bridal March" but it broke. My best friend's mom and my friend Cathy stepped up to the piano and started playing without skipping a beat. I had never seen my momma in a dress before. She looked so pretty. I can still see her standing there. I don't think she could believe that I was actually getting married. It was a beautiful day.

It was the beginning of a new chapter in my life and I was getting ready to find out that things weren't going to be easy. James was 29 when God saved him. He was 10 years older than me. He had gotten saved, filled with God's Spirit and married all within 6 months. He had been delivered from drugs and alcohol but had a lot of rough edges that needed smoothing. I wasn't "all that" either; I was almost 2 years old in the Lord at 19 ½ years old. This is where you are supposed to laugh. We had many struggles, which is common when two people join with different backgrounds, habits and each of us carrying baggage, along with the fact that we didn't even know each other. I quickly found out that James's perception of women was not Biblical. He was very authoritative and many times verbally abusive and possessive. There came a time that I had my clothes packed, not knowing exactly where I was going to go, but I didn't want our testimony to my mom and dad tainted. Listen friends, I will never forget hearing these words so clear, "Diana how many times have I forgiven you?" It was so powerful it stopped me in my tracks. I unpacked my bags and knew that when I said "I do", I was in for the long haul.

I knew what the Word of God said about divorce, and I wanted to be a testimony to my family and to others that

God can work things out. We shouldn't give up when things are tough. I mostly would talk to my mother-in-law about our fights, because she loved James and loved me like I was her daughter. I was afraid others would judge us or judge James and I didn't want that. I would defend her in many ways as James had a difficult time in even knowing how to treat his mom. This was not something that I or anyone could fix, but God is the Potter and we are the clay. There are times we must go through the fire to get where we need to be.

PERSONAL INSIGHT

I am committed to my marriage. Vows are sacred to me. I have rarely promised my daughter anything, because I never know what may come up. The only thing I promise her is that I will always love her. I made a vow to my husband and I will do all I can to keep that vow. Ladies, as I discussed earlier, you must find someone who is running after God just as hard as you are. James loved God. He had been delivered from so much, and I am so thankful for all that God has done in his heart. One thing to look for as you begin to consider dating is how a man treats his mother. How does he talk to his mom? What does he do to show his respect and love for her? These are important questions. James loved his mother very much. He just had a few issues with the way he spoke to her. He took care of her in many ways and tried to help meet her needs. We took her to church for many years. What I've seen in how he took care of his mom is the way he takes care of me, but he exhibits the same issues with how he communicates. This doesn't mean things can't work, but it does mean there will be trials ahead. How committed are you to weather those storms? We are examples of this.

Although I have felt like my heart was going to break, I have never wanted to hurt my husband, and I didn't want anyone judging him. I had a physician to ask me in his grumpy old way one morning, "Why are you always smiling? It's got to be a personality defect?" Little did he know I had cried myself to sleep the night before because of how I had been treated. I know my husband has a heart for God and that is the main reason we have survived the storms. Anger is one letter away from danger. It is ok to be angry but there must come a time when those who deal with this issue realize their need for help and surrender this emotion entirely to God. James is tender towards me. He will do things for me that show me his love. He tells me he adores me, and that I am the best woman he's ever known. He has beautiful qualities. He is a giver; he has rubbed my feet countless hours over the years. He is thoughtful. He is a faithful husband and a protector. Never knowing what may cause him to explode is an area that has put a strain in both our relationship and his relationship with Kayla. But he loves us enough that he is willing to partake in family counseling.

This will be a blessing to our home as we strive to love each other the way Jesus has called us to love.

God tells us that adultery is not just the act of committing adultery but it is the thought and continual lusting over someone. There was a time in our marriage when things were really rocky and the enemy knew I was vulnerable. I had been promoted in a position and worked with another Christian male. Our jobs were to go from facility to facility to work with teams. As time went on, there was an obvious attraction, at least on my end. Husbands and wives, do not ever put yourself in a situation, especially when you are weak, that could cause you to jeopardize your relationship with your spouse or with God. This is setting yourself up for unnecessary pain. Thankfully, I had enough courage to talk to James about what I was encountering and asked him to pray with me. I would also do all I could to limit being alone with this individual, because I knew the tactics of the enemy, and I did not want to bring shame to God or my husband.

Ladies, if you compare your husband to others then you are opening the door of temptation and destruction in your marriage. The comparison game is destructive no matter if it's comparing yourself to someone else, your husband to another man, or your family to others.

It also doesn't help when there are other issues in the marriage such as working separate shifts, sick and aging parents, etc. James worked first shift and I worked second shift. Additionally, my mom had become very ill. We hardly saw each other and the time we did have together was not the best during these difficult days.

One of my main goals in life was to see my family saved. God had put a burden on my heart for my family's salvation. I believed that God had given me a *Rhema* word that He would save them, but it would not come without a price.

According to the Advanced Training Institute, there are two primary Greek words used to describe Scripture. These words are translated as *word* in the New Testament. The first word, *logos*, refers to primarily to the "total inspired Word of God and to Jesus, Who is the living *Logos*." The second Greek word used to describe Scripture is *rhema*. In this sense, *rhema* describes a word that is spoken and literally means 'an utterance.' "A *rhema* is a verse or a portion of Scripture that the Holy Spirit brings to our attention with application to a current situation or need for direction."[3]

I bought every tape I could find on salvation. I would listen to them as I sewed swatches on production at Fabric Services. I listened to preaching for hours. God was preparing me for a time when I wasn't going to have the opportunity to saturate myself in His Word. I would pass cassette tapes around to others when I felt

---

[3] Advanced Training Institute (2016). Retrieved from http://atii.org/what-is-a-rhema/

impressed to do so. I would be sewing and crying. Everyone was just used to seeing me cry I think. I would be so touched by what I would hear. There were lives that were touched through my obedience. One coworker gave her heart to Jesus in the bathroom. I have run into her a few times and she is still serving God today. As a matter of fact, as I was working on this book, I ran into her at a Japanese restaurant. She shared a few things she had been through but proclaimed that God is still number one in her life. It was as if God was encouraging me to stay on track. I had another dear friend who called me one day to let me know she had given her heart to Jesus. I have lost contact with her, but I am trusting that what was sown in her heart, God is able to keep. I would sit at that machine and have dreams of doing something great for the Kingdom of God. I would see myself preaching to a large crowd and winning people to Jesus. I had this passion burning inside of me.

The owners of Fabric Services loved me. We went to church together and they were always so good to me and those who worked for them. They would buy gifts at Christmas and allow us to choose by seniority. They would also give us monetary gifts. I asked them if I could say a few words before picking out gifts one year; they were so kind and willing to allow me to do so. I was so excited but extremely nervous as I had never spoken in front of people before. The Lord helped me to bring a message of the Cross to a group of 30 individuals that day. Many responded with raised hands when I asked if there was a need for prayer. God was doing a work in my life as I walked in obedience.

CHAPTER SIX

The first 3 years of my new life with Jesus, my husband and the church were really enjoyable. I grew at a phenomenal pace, and felt like I was impacting lives around me, but there came a time when I felt an urgency for my family like never before. I listened to a message by Jentezen Franklin about winning your family to Christ. I heard in my spirit something that burned deep to the core: "You were a stone taken up out of your family, cleaned up and placed back in the center to make an eternal difference in their lives."

I wanted to change the world for Christ, but who was going to do that for my family? I knew no one else could make intercession for them like I could. I didn't want them to die and go to hell. I had learned that fasting was key to seeing difficult prayers answered. I tried at that time to make fasting a regular part of my life; I would try to fast one to two full days a week. There were times I would be led to fast for longer periods of time. The longest I had gone was five days on a complete fast. The Word of God says that some things will only come through prayer and fasting (Mark 9:29, NIV).

I can't remember the day or the exact month, but I will never forget the burden I had for my family after leaving a church service. I pleaded with God to save my family. My heart was so heavy I could not bear it. I prayed a prayer that would change the course of my life, as I knelt at the end of my bed crying and wailing. I warn you not to pray this prayer unless you truly mean it and are prepared to weather the storm. I prayed, "God, no matter what it takes please save my family. Please don't let them die without You!"

In February 1995, I had planned something special for my parent's 25th anniversary. I had learned a lot about fellowship and parties from being around my church family, and I wanted my parents to experience a surprise party. I had a special video made from old pictures, bought decorations, had a special cake made and had invited Robert and Ricky to share the special occasion. Unfortunately, things hadn't turned out the way I had planned. My mom was supposed to be at her mother's house but she stayed at home that day. You can imagine the disappointment I felt. Robert came but Ricky missed being there. You could smell the stench of alcohol on my brother as we all sat in the living room to watch the video.

My brother had a relationship with daddy like I had with momma. I can only think in his heart he wished daddy would just love him for who he was. I could tell this was a source of some resentment coming from my mom as she favored Robert in a way. A picture of Robert came on the screen where he was being silly. Daddy said, "You can just see the devil in that boy's eyes!" My brother ran out the door crying. I asked daddy, "Why did you have to say that?" Daddy ran out the door behind him. Momma and I stared out the back window crying as we watched daddy grab him and hug him. I had never seen my parents break like that before. It was a pivotal moment in their relationship. Daddy began to soften up towards Robert. He started helping him out, allowing him to drive his vehicle when he needed help. This was a much-needed intervention because of what was going to happen.

The following year, James and I happened to close on a little three-bedroom house on his birthday. He brought boxes home one day saying we were going to buy a home. I hadn't thought much about it, because we were struggling to get out of debt that he was in before we got married. (Another word of advice: Couples, seek godly counsel regarding finances before you are married. This is one of the major reasons for divorces).

I was thankful for the roof over our head even though it was tin and covered what look like a barn. A little dramatic but we had no air and the only heat source we had was a wood stove that would dry out our sinuses like crazy. When it rained, the water would turn muddy. I tried not to let those things bother me. I painted the walls to try to make it look homey. I remembered saying to James, "Yeah right!" He had more faith concerning this than I did. There wasn't a lot that we could get within our budget at the time but the little house we have has turned out to be our home for almost 20 years now. Our church family gave us a house warming party. We were so grateful for the love that was shown to us during this time.

That May I was summoned for jury duty. I was visiting my parents when Robert came over. He asked me, "Sissy, do you have any money I can borrow?" I hesitated to give him money, because I didn't want him to buy alcohol with it. He was hungry and needed some gas money. I'm so glad I gave him some money that day. June came and James and I went to Perry Stone's yearly camp meeting at Heritage USA. We went to the Friday night service. Saturday, I tried to find Robert to remind him that Sunday was Father's day and for him not to forget daddy. He had moved so I wasn't sure of his exact whereabouts. I drove around the mobile home park searching hard for any signs of him. I saw someone I used to work with and she knew Robert. She said he had gone to the lake with some guys. I was torn between trying to find him and going to camp meeting. I felt like I was the one who tried to bring love and unity to our family. I didn't want to miss camp meeting because this was something I really enjoyed doing with my husband. The trip wasn't peaceful and I didn't receive anything from the meeting that night. It wasn't because of Perry Stone, but because of the principalities of the air. I felt such an oppression that I sat with my arms folded.

We ended up getting in an argument on the way back home.

I was thankful we had bought the tapes from the week. I listened to those recordings on Monday and decided to fast for my family on Tuesday. James tried calling work to find me. I can't remember what took me so long to get home. When I got home, I found my 6-foot 2-inch husband in the floor crying like I had never seen him before. I was afraid to ask him what was wrong. I did not anticipate that it could be anything terrible. He got up and wrapped his arms around me and told me he had just seen on the news that emergency crews had pulled Robert out of Lake Hickory. They had called my parents to come identify him. My momma was the one who had to look at his body that had been in the water for four days. His chin had burst open from where he had gotten hurt when he was a little toddler. I felt as if I didn't hear any of that. It wasn't true. It just couldn't be.

I found out that Robert had been on a boat with some people my husband used to party with and he said they were bad news. James still to this day believes there was foul play involved. Robert had just gotten paid and they had been drinking. I was devastated. I didn't know what to do and I sure didn't understand.   I knew and believed in my heart that God was going to save my family. I also knew what the scriptures said about drunkards, they shall not inherit the Kingdom of God (1 Corinthians 6:10).

The story was that Robert had been swimming and he told the guys if they were ready to go he would just swim to a friend's house in the cove. He never made it. I rode with my parents to the funeral home. My momma said to me, "I don't know how you turned out like you did." I had been a Christian for five years at that time, trying hard to prove myself to my parents that the experience I had 5 years earlier was real, that I had been changed. I told her it was God. I can see my daddy on his knees at the bench in the funeral home, weeping...crying and praying so hard. I had never seen my daddy pray. I knelt beside him and prayed and found myself praying in the Holy Spirit, because I didn't know what to pray.

A few days later momma asked me if James had ever hit me. She told me Robert had talked to her about the way James treated me. We had let him stay with us for a little while when we were still at the "barn". It probably wasn't a good idea because of the problems we were having. Robert told momma, "If he ever lays a hand on sissy, I will kill him." We weren't really used to being talked to the way James talked to me and the way he had spoken to my brothers. My mom was tough but we very seldom heard daddy talk to momma in an ill manner. It would upset me beyond what I could express in words. I never cared what my brothers did or didn't do...I loved them unconditionally. I will say that this was one of the first major regrets that my husband had experienced in our relationship. James "wished he had treated my brother better." This was a good sign, but this is a situation where you don't want to have to learn the hard way. Once someone is gone, there are no more chances.

My momma was rough but James was on a totally different level. Momma wanted to make sure that I wasn't getting hit. I assured her that I wasn't. I didn't feel comfortable talking to momma about these things. I was on a mission to see her saved, and I didn't want her to see the bad. I wanted her to see the good in both of us and not our faults. I took all my troubles about my hubby to his momma, because I knew she would pray for us and lift us both up to the Father. She was indeed my best friend. I didn't realize just how rough hubby was before we took our vows, but I saw and heard him pray, and I knew his heart was for God.

PERSONAL INSIGHT

I by no means think it is ever ok to be abused emotionally or physically, or to live in a situation where you are beaten down constantly. I do believe if someone is trying and they are repentant that it adds something different to the equation, understanding that true repentance brings change. It is a very sensitive subject for me, as I am certain for many others who may be reading this. I have cried more tears than I have ever wanted. According to Matthew, "Peter asked Jesus, 'How many times shall I forgive my brother who sins against me, seven times?' Jesus replies, 'No seventy times seven'" (Matthew 18:21-22). This is huge. That is four hundred and ninety times. We cannot do this within ourselves. We must have the Holy Spirit working full time in our lives to be able to fulfill this commandment. If we are willing to do this for those we love how much more should we for those who do not love us?

It is always best to seek Godly counsel for these issues. The worldly and carnal-minded will always tell you what the ears want to hear. We must hear what God is telling each of us in our own individual situations. You must find someone you trust, someone you know will take your situation before the throne of God, and not to Sally Sue who spends most her time gossiping about everything and everyone...and enjoys it. This can be difficult as one needs discernment to be able to determine who you can trust. Believe me, I have been the victim of "a wolf in sheep's clothing" and it is not fun. You will hear more about that a little later. 1

Corinthians 7:16 says, "Don't you know that husbands may be saved because of you?" I believe this is meant for those who got married before they found Jesus, and for those who may have led a very rough life before God saved them. God does not want you to choose a mate with whom you will be unequally yoked on major life beliefs and issues.

James and I did not have much discussion about anything. We were moved by each other's passion we had for God. Find out about who you are going to be spending the rest of your life with; even if you do or don't, God's Word tells us that a vow should not be easily broken. Marriages are sacred. Spouses are not like cars that can be traded. Pray and keep praying until you have heard from heaven. I am not saying that James and I weren't meant to be. What I am saying is that when we spend time in His presence we cannot help but be changed. This is the answer for every struggle, every trial, and every hurt.

CHAPTER SEVEN

James and I were doing the bus ministry at our church and had been for some time. I was so excited about this ministry. The children loved James. I would try to go out on Saturdays and encourage the kiddos to be at church the next morning. We had managed to grow to the point where we were making 2 trips to get all the kiddos. After the death of my brother, I could not continue. I was struggling trying to find answers. Many would speak encouraging words to me, reminding me that the thief on the cross did not pray a long prayer, he just said "remember me." I did learn that drowning was a very slow and painful process. Robert had been to church with his best friend several times. He had a sister who prayed and fasted for him. No one really knew what I was asking of God. I didn't know what to expect. I wondered why I didn't have enough faith or enough power to say, "Rise up in the name of Jesus and he be resurrected." What could I have done differently? I know I could have prayed and fasted more. Before James and I left for vacation one Sunday an individual was sitting behind me in church. She had written a note and handed it to me. I placed it in my Bible. It said, "Your answer is coming saith the Lord." I had not told anyone about my prayer: "Please God, show me that Robert made it to heaven and that he cried out to you in his final breath."

We found ourselves at the beach. Being around the water made me uncomfortable. James and I were out pretty far in the ocean just goofing around when a wave came and knocked his wedding ring off his finger. He kept going down under the water trying to get it. I told him it was gone. The tide was strong and it was impossible for him to find that ring. After a while, we left to go grab something to eat. Several hours passed before we went back to the same area. The tide was out by now. We were sitting in our chairs and James saw a gentleman with a metal detector. He asked me, "Do you think that guy has found my wedding ring?" I thought, "Really? I know he just didn't ask me that." I can relate to how Sarah felt when Abraham told her she would have a son at her age in Genesis 18:12. It's different but the same principal. Impossible!!

James went down to talk with the man. He agreed to search for the ring. James came back and sat with me. A little later, the man beckoned James to meet him. He asked him what his ring looked like. James described the ring and after digging close to two feet this man had found my husband's wedding ring! I can still see my husband throwing up his hands to Heaven and praising God. Yep, right there on the beach in front of everybody. I don't believe in coincidences or luck and the Bible doesn't teach it either. As Psalms 37:23 (KJV) says, "The steps of a righteous man are ordered by the Lord." James proceeded to share with me, "Honey, when I realized I lost my ring, I prayed to God and asked him that if Robert had called out to Him and made it to heaven, to please let me find my ring." James had even forgotten about the prayer when he realized he wasn't able to find it on his own. A peace came over me that I could not explain. Although the human side of me tried to find flaw in this situation by asking James many times, "Are you sure you prayed that prayer?" I could not deny that God had divinely and strategically aligned our paths with someone from another state at that very time. The worldly minded will say, "Well isn't it a small world?" NO! We just serve a BIG, BIG God! I am reminded how powerful this story is when my husband was helping a friend with his yard and the ring fell off his finger again. He was never able to find the ring in that small yard. Only God could think of something so amazing!!

I wish I could say that I moved on with my life with purpose, that we picked the bus ministry back up and went on with our lives as we knew it. Although I felt peace in my heart, I still had a difficult time with my brother's death.

One day I decided to try to find the guys that Robert was with the day he died. Alone. James did not know I had gone until afterwards, which wasn't the smartest thing to do, and I knew how upset he would be with me. I wanted to see their eyes and hear what they had to say. I can't remember everything that was said. I was right; James was not happy with me. He majorly views himself as my protector, and did not like that I put myself in a position where I could have been hurt. But I just had to do it. I think that both of the men that were with him when he died have subsequently died from drug-related events. This does not make me happy. It saddens me.

My momma was a mess. Here she was dealing with the images of her baby boy who had drowned. I would check on her frequently. As a coping mechanism, I found it was easier if I stayed busy. I decided to go back to school starting the fall of that year. James got angry with me. We were at the Fresh Air Galaxy when I got out of the car while he was in the store and just started walking home. That was my stubbornness coming out. I enrolled in 2 courses against his wishes. This was heavy for me because not only was I working full time, I was helping my husband deliver newspapers on top of trying to make sure my parents were okay. We had picked up that extra side job to try to get ahead and pay off some bills. How did this happen especially since I hated it so much growing up? We made decent money, but James was getting worn out. He wasn't sleeping well and actually had not slept well since we married. We had all been affected by Robert's tragic death. It wasn't going to get any easier. I noticed that I had allowed myself to start watching things that I would have never watched before, specifically a show called *90210*. I was getting my nails done a few years ago and that show came on. I had a flashback to these days, and I couldn't believe that I would allow such ungodliness in my spirit: adultery, fornication, lying, gossip, and immorality. My heart was towards God and I wanted His blessings on my life. I removed those habits as I surrendered my ways to Him.

PERSONAL INSIGHT

Busyness was a way of dealing with my brother's death, in spite of the blessing God had given me through the wedding ring experience. I was overwhelmed with life and seeing my mom decline mentally and emotionally. I was trying to keep it all together. If you have experienced painful tragedies in your life, I highly recommend grief counseling with a Christian counselor or talking to someone who has been through the same things but exhibits a strong relationship with God. It doesn't mean God is any less powerful or that you are any less spiritual. It is a healthy way to deal with unexpected deaths or tragedies. God is our "Wonderful Counselor" (Isaiah

9:6). I believe He has all power to heal our emotions when we seek Him.

I continued with school until 1998 when I received an acceptance letter for the nursing program. James and I did not have the money for me to quit work and we didn't have enough faith that God would supply what we needed. I gave up on the thoughts of getting my nursing degree and started looking for employment elsewhere. I realized later it was certainly not God's timing. I was starting to hurt badly in my wrists and shoulders from sewing on production. God had opened doors for me with a job closer to home working in a cable plant. It was here that I met some amazing individuals, made some dear friends, and became pregnant with my precious baby girl. There were many trials along the way during my time here. I tried going back to school for a different major, Accounting. Although I made an A in the class, I realized it wasn't for me. It just didn't make sense to me.

During the 4 years I was at this manufacturing plant, I was challenged to share the love of God with others. I also learned how to deal with someone who suffered from Bipolar Disorder (prior to this time, I had no knowledge of this disorder). For some reason, I seem to attract this population group. This individual did not like me. Thankfully, I went through the correct process to deal with the issues which helped me receive a promotion later. I started out on second shift, which was tough on our marriage, but in a way, was good because we fought less. I missed going to church on Wednesday nights. I remember having deep conversations with a few individuals regarding faith and theology that would leave one or the other frustrated. I enjoyed these conversations because it pushed me to study God's Word more deeply. I had the opportunity to move to first shift and would meet some more cool people with whom I could share my faith.

My mom wanted to move. I worked on getting their house ready, painting every room. Daddy didn't want to move, but he would do anything for my momma. He loved her. I never heard him yell at her. If he did I have blocked it from my memory. Momma was usually the one upset with daddy, but she was going deeper and deeper into a pit of depression. During this time, we had an evangelist preaching at our church. I always invited others to church with me and I must have invited momma to come, at least that is what she told me. He was gifted with the prophetic word. Lives were being changed. She called me one night and told me that she had gotten ready to come to church and had waited for me but I never came to get her. I do not recall her ever telling me she would go. I cried and cried. I know we have the ability to win others to Christ by living out our faith, but there is something about literally hearing the preached Word of God that will stir up the soul; I had missed the opportunity. How could I have done that?

She was not handling Robert's death well at all. She did not know the peace that comes through knowing Jesus.

I shared our story from the beach with both my parents. I could tell it relieved my daddy. I remember him asking Pastor Miles if he would pray for Robert. The sad thing is that once we die there are no more chances, unless you are one of the few people that God decides to breathe His breath into and bring you back to life. If you are one of those fortunate individuals, you better believe you are meant to share your story so that others may be saved from an eternal hell.

I had someone tell me once that he had died and gone to hell. He said that he was given another chance to live and he knew God had saved him but he "didn't want to be a Bible thumper and force his beliefs on others." I shared with him I didn't think he had a choice because his life was spared for a reason. I hope I was able to encourage him to write a book or spend more time telling others that hell is real and that they don't want to go there.

My parents moved to a place in the mountain area 45 minutes from where I lived. This put a major strain on me. When I would get there, I could not stay long because I would have to leave to get to work. I found that momma was getting more and more dependent on medication and was not in a right frame of mind when I would visit. Between worrying about her and my daddy who was having to drive so much more to get his routes done, I was having a hard time trying to find a happy place.

CHAPTER EIGHT

It was almost New Years of 2000. I left work early that day feeling oppressed and not knowing exactly why. I never missed work or left work. When I got home, there was a message on my machine. It was daddy. His message said, "They have taken your momma to Grace Hospital. The EMS workers said she was dead but they were able to bring her back." I cried and prayed all the way to Morganton, "PLEASE GOD DON'T LET MY MOMMA DIE. PLEASE DON'T LET HER DIE WITHOUT YOU!!" She was not eating and she had been living off anti-depressants and anti-anxiety medications. She was anemic. Brother Miles met me at the hospital and prayed with her. God spared my momma's life that day. I told my parents they had to move back closer to me so I could help take care of them. The drive was too hard on my daddy and momma was being left alone too long. They were dying on that mountain.

I found a house for rent about 3 minutes away from me. We were able to move them closer to home. I helped daddy with his paper route and bills while I worked full-time and tried to keep my own home in order. James was put on the back burner. It wasn't supposed to be this way, but this was my life and I had no other choice. I received a call at work one day that momma had been rushed to the hospital. She had severe bleeding that turned out to be a rectal tumor. Had they not performed emergency surgery it would have ruptured and killed her then. It was during this time that my momma realized she didn't want to die. I told her she still had a daughter, a son, and my daddy who loved her and we needed her. She had filed for disability several times and had been denied. I had been praying that God would allow her to get this much-needed benefit. My parents had lost everything they had worked so hard for all their life.

I remember hearing someone say a snide remark about a patient who was 48 and had Medicaid. This individual or nobody has any right to talk about something they know nothing about. No one saw what my parents went through but me; and no one knows what anyone else endures either. Yes, there are those who abuse the system. These people are the ones who make it hard for those who do deserve assistance when they need it and should be ashamed of themselves.

I wrote a letter to the judge pleading my mother's case and asked the question, "Does someone have to be on their deathbed before they can receive help?" It wasn't as if my mother had not worked her entire life. I would go to the local post office to check the mail for my daddy. It was getting harder for him to get around. Both my parents had endured 3 back surgeries and they suffered from chronic pain. Nevertheless, my daddy would not quit working. He took pride in taking care of momma. One day when checking the mail, I saw a package. I opened it and saw that momma's disability had been approved. Now she still had spunk in her. I walked in her bedroom and turned off the television without asking. She told me to turn it back on. I took advantage of the fact that she was not as mobile as she once was and I had a preaching session. I gave them a little sermon and made sure they knew that every good gift comes from above. I remember momma telling me, "I don't know what we would do without you." For the first time in my life, I remember momma telling me that she loved me. She had probably told me before but that day it really stood out. I promised momma as long as God gave me physical strength I would do all I could for her and daddy.

After 6 months of living in the rental property, the state was talking about paving a new road that would become McDonald Parkway. Someone had come to talk to my parents and offered them

$14,000 to find a house under $60,000. We told the people that my parents were just renters, but they still offered my parents this amount of money. My daddy found a little house they would soon call home. It wasn't much, but it was theirs, and I made sure they understood that God had provided for them. I knew in my heart they could not deny this was the hand of God.

I was working second shift in July of 2002. I had been promoted, gone through training and was back on second shift rotation. I stopped by to check on momma after work. Daddy was already gone on his route. My heart began to beat fast which is a common symptom when God is asking me to do something. I felt the Spirit dealing with me to talk to momma about her soul. It wasn't an easy task, but I believed God had prepared her heart for this time. She looked like a concentration camp victim. She had a PEG tube in her stomach so she could receive nutrition. She looked so helpless lying there with her big eyes staring up at me. I knelt beside her and I looked into her eyes and asked, "Momma do you know if you would go to Heaven if something happened to you?" "No," she said. I asked her, "Would you like to know for sure that you would go to Heaven?" She nodded her head, "Yes." I prompted her to repeat after me. I began to pray and momma just listened, but I stopped and asked her to repeat after me. That night momma received Jesus as her Lord and Savior. She told me she had wanted to do this but "never knew what to say." I assured her that night her name was written in a special book called the Lamb's Book of Life. I wrote, "Thank you Jesus for saving my momma" on my white board and I still have it in my kitchen.

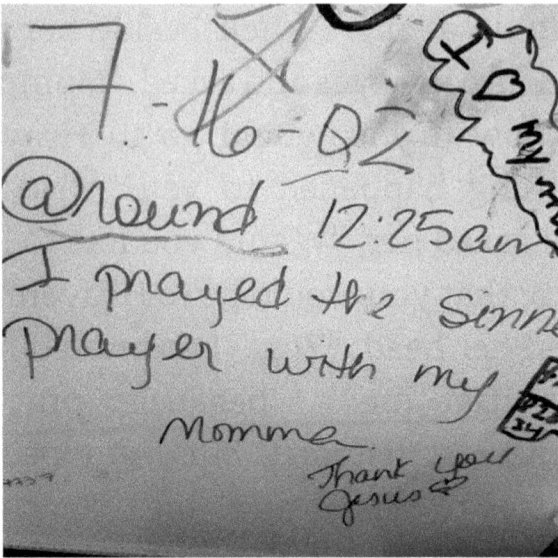

7-16-02
@round 12:25am
I prayed the sinn[er]
Prayer with my
Momma
Thank you
Jesus

My mom had been in and out of the hospital and I never knew when I would get the news that she would not get to come home. There were times I would wait countless hours in the emergency room because no one in the ER knew how to place a Dobhoff tube when hers would get clogged up.

I remember being at their house when a home health nurse came out to show my daddy how to use the PEG tube she had surgically placed to provide momma with nutrition. She was such a hateful nurse. I remember telling myself, "If I had the opportunity to become a nurse, I would never treat anyone like she treated my momma." I was livid. I found out later, after I had become a home health nurse, that they could have been offered a hospital bed along with a few other things that would have made it easier on them. Momma stayed so sick. She would throw up all the time and I had to try to find a way to give her a bath which was not the easiest thing to do when she could not get up. I remember daddy calling James one night when momma had fallen in the tub. Daddy couldn't get her up by himself with his hurt back. I can only imagine how my momma felt, as private as she had always been. I had so little extra time trying to work, helping daddy with his route, their finances and sitting with momma at the hospital and doctors. I just needed someone to help me and there was no one. The sickness, pain and devastation was more than I could bear at times. My dad wasn't in good health and I was trying to do all I could to help him.

CHAPTER NINE

One day on our way to church, we were in James' little station wagon and he was going around a curve to pick up his mom and sister. I got nauseous and told him I was going to have to sit in the back seat because I didn't know what was going on. After dealing with nausea for several days, I decided that it wouldn't hurt to take a pregnancy test. At the beginning of the year, James had me thinking about having a baby. We had been married nine years. He started smiling at the babies at church and began entertaining the thought. I had not really thought about having kiddos. I did not want to bring a baby into the world if I did not have my husband's 100% buy-in. That's all I could think about for a while. We would try to get pregnant and I got depressed because I was having a difficult time. Spring came and I had to snap out of it because momma had to have surgery for rectal cancer. I received a call that my daddy had hit a telephone pole while delivering newspapers during the night. Daddy was in critical care for a week. I didn't know if he was going to make it. I wasn't sure how I could continue under all this stress and pressure. I stayed with momma, ran daddy's route, tried to take care of all I could in our home and go see daddy every day. My aunt Barbara came to see daddy and brought him a little book with the Gospel in it. Pastor Miles had been called away to help a church in Mooresville. I did not have time to build a relationship with the current Pastor at the church. I rationed momma's medicine out to her and only gave it to her when it was time. I told momma and daddy that when I had the baby they were going to have to stop smoking. This was a huge issue with my parents. They had always smoked like freight trains, one of the major reasons why I had trouble breathing growing up. I am so glad that when I tried smoking I didn't like it. I didn't like breathing in all the smoke while I was staying with my momma. I thanked God for sparing my daddy and giving him another chance. I was getting weak and tired.

I was so sick during my pregnancy. It was not the normal sickness; it was magnified. I threw up all the time and James would hold the bucket for me. In my third trimester, he made the mistake of getting mad and asking me when I was going to stop throwing up, as if I could control it. I would carry a cup with me when I went to collect money from my daddy's stores on Saturdays. I tried to maintain exercise but just couldn't tolerate lots of motion. I would get sick with healthy foods but could eat cake and not get sick, so I still managed to gain an unhealthy amount of weight. In November, at 6 months pregnant, I received another call at 4:30 in the morning. Daddy had fallen asleep and had driven across all four lanes of Springs Road and his van was turned upside down in a field where it had gone off the road. Daddy had miraculously gotten out alive and walked to Food Lion across the street to call me. I had the stress of daddy working but not physically being able to, while worrying about him getting killed in the middle of the night.

My life was a whirlwind. I kept hearing God will never give us more than we can bear, but I was beginning to doubt that. Have you been there? Whatever you do, DON'T GIVE UP!! Keep pressing forward! Ask for prayer and try to surround yourself with like-minded individuals who believe in the power of prayer. My prayer is that I will always be an answer to someone's prayer. Let me be the one to offer my assistance, let me be the one to share the good news to a wayward child that a grandma is interceding for. Let me be His hands and feet in some way.

PERSONAL INSIGHT

During my first years of my walk with God while we lived at "the barn," we had a neighbor that I had connected with (I think over makeup or something similar). I began to build her trust. Her husband was sick and he was bedridden. She had asked if I could sit with him, for what reason I can't remember. In my mind, I felt I would be condemned if I did not go to church that Wednesday night, and I told her I wasn't going to be able to sit with him. The Holy Spirit convicted me beyond anything I can even express to you. In Luke 14:5 (NIV) the Bible says, "Then he asked them, 'If one of you has a child or an ox that falls into a well on the Sabbath day, will you not immediately pull it out?'" I learned a valuable lesson from this. One night before my momma gotten so sick, she asked me to go to the fair with her. It had always been my desire to "do" things with momma. She wanted me to be with her and I turned her down because I felt that I would be condemned going to the fair instead of going to church that night. Yes, I understand that Jesus said, "If you love your mother and father more than me you aren't worthy of being mine," Matthew 10:37; but you must look at the big picture. This could have been an opportunity to show her God's love; Jesus already knew my heart was for Him and that I was loyal to Him. I had always wanted to be really close with momma, yet I failed to grasp this opportunity. Legalism kept me from being God's hands in both these situations, and if I had the chance to go back I would choose differently.

According to Wikipedia "**Legalism** (or nomism), in Christian theology, is the act of putting the law above the gospel by establishing requirements for salvation beyond repentance and faith in Jesus Christ and reducing the broad, inclusive, and general precepts of the Bible to narrow and rigid moral codes. It is an over-emphasis of discipline of conduct, or legal ideas, usually implying an allegation of misguided, rigour, pride, superficiality, the neglect of mercy, and ignorance of the grace of God or emphasizing the letter of law at the expense of the spirit. Legalism is alleged against any view that obedience to law, not faith in God's grace, is the pre-eminent principle of redemption. On the Biblical viewpoint that redemption is not earned by works, but that obedient faith is required to enter and remain in the redeemed state."[4]

Getting back to the story...some dear friends I made at work, gave me a baby shower: Robin and Lisa and their daughters, Kelsey and Courtney. Both these ladies hold a special place in my heart for they both know all too well and can

---

[4] *Legalism (theology).* Wikipedia. Retrieved November 30, 2016 from
https://en.wikipedia.org/wiki/Legalism_(theology)

relate to the pain from tragic events in their own lives. Robin continues to be an encourager in my life and has actually encouraged me to write. Momma was too sick to even be excited for me. Daddy was trying to survive with the pain he was in and trying to take care of momma. Kayla was due on February 21, 2002. The 21st was a good number for us. James, my brother Ricky, James' momma, and I were all born on the 21st and February 21st was my parent's anniversary. James and I wanted to get married on the 21st but couldn't wait. We were married 7 days earlier on the 14th of May, which was the same day his brother and wife married. I started having difficulty with major swelling. I had a midwife and anticipated a natural delivery but when the doctor assessed me in the hospital he said I would not be able to have the baby naturally. Imagine me not having hips wide enough to bear a child! My midwife was at another hospital but instructed the nurses to have me push. Kayla was not going to make it to the 21$^{st.}$ I had pushed for over an hour. She was going into fetal distress so we were rushed to surgery for a C-section. I remember the anesthesiologist being so rude. I am so sensitive to medications, and I could not think straight to answer her questions. I finally heard a sound from my baby but it was a short "whaaa." She didn't cry. I was so worried but she was ok. She looked at her daddy like she could strangle him. She was not a happy camper. I guess I wouldn't be either if had to go through what she had gone through.

I remember the day we brought her home in her little Winnie the Pooh outfit that my aunt Judy had bought her. I would just sit and cry as I looked at how beautiful my baby was and how unworthy I felt that God would bless me with such a gift.

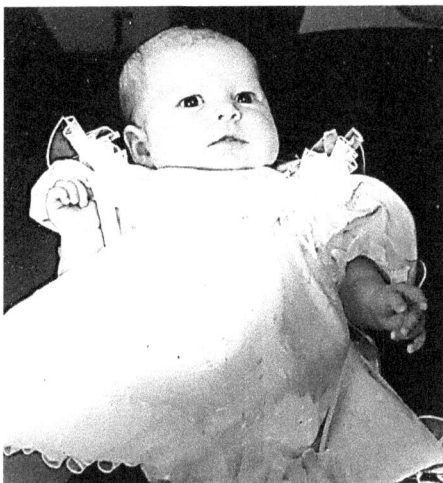

My friend always told me that I would better understand the love that God has for me when I had a child. I couldn't understand that concept because of the love I had for my family. Momma told me something I will always treasure; she said, "I didn't know if you would make a good momma but you are." I had been mentored by a woman of God named Sandy. She was such a good mother. I would baby sit for her and Sam when their boys were little. She nursed little Kyle and I couldn't understand or fathom this concept. I didn't have this kind of nurturing growing up, but God allowed me to see an example of how to raise a baby with a healthy way of thinking. I decided to nurse Kayla, and it was one of the best decisions I could have chosen for her. A nurse had to come out to our house to help. I had become depressed over the thoughts that I may not have the opportunity to nurse because I came down with mastitis with a fever of 105. I didn't give up easily. I was able to nurse Kayla for 14 months. It was a beautiful bonding experience.

Shortly after I had Kayla, the plant where I worked started laying off employees. I found out that they were going to pay for education through a bill the government had passed and I asked them to lay me off. I was told no. I took that as a compliment, but I desperately needed a change. That August they did another lay off and I was given a severance package. I applied for nursing school and was told that the state would not pay for nursing. They said it was too hard to get into the program. I had visited every surrounding school. All programs were on a first come, first serve basis except the local community college which was competitive. I wrote a letter to the state giving them my information. I told them that I had taken almost all the non-core classes and had a 4.0 GPA and was as competitive as anyone else applying. I received a letter that stated if I could get an acceptance letter by a certain date then they would pay for the program. I worked diligently during this time to get as many of the courses completed as I could with A's to strengthen my chances. This gave me some time to spend with Kayla as well as continue to run two households and help daddy with his route. I was blessed to have a dear friend, Becky who would help me watch Kayla so I could go collect from the stores without having to take her with me. Momma seemed to be gaining weight. She loved it when I would make her rice and gravy. I tried to cook what I could for her especially when she could eat. I bought machines with filters to put in their house to try to get rid of as much smoke as I could to try to protect Kayla, but it wasn't enough. Momma had been hospitalized when Kayla was a few months old. Her PEG tube became infected with MRSA. I didn't know what MRSA was at this time, but learned really quickly it wasn't good when a nurse scolded me for not having a gown on while I was visiting momma.

On May 17, 2003 I was on student break for about a week, which was God's grace towards me, because He knew what I was getting ready to go through. Kayla was 15 months old. I got a call from daddy to get to the hospital. Daddy could not handle things well and didn't want to talk to the doctor. The doctor pulled me aside and told me momma's liver was failing and it was just a matter of time. I couldn't believe it. Momma was gaining weight and was looking better. I was going to sit with her during break to show her videos from Kayla's first birthday party. She couldn't die. She wasn't supposed to be here. They informed us she was not a candidate for a liver transplant. Her liver was failing from acetaminophen toxicity.   Daddy could not take seeing momma in this condition.   I stayed with her most of the time leaving late at night and coming back in early. During this time, James was not being sensitive. He wanted me to take care of Kayla when my momma had been given a death sentence.   The Pastor was out of town. My brother had not been up to see momma. He and daddy seemed to be at odds all the time. I can't help but to think how my momma missed seeing him. Momma loved Ricky so much. I was pretty much at a breaking point. Momma was in ICU and the nurses had just given her two units of blood. I saw momma sit up and regurgitate all the blood. I screamed, "Please someone help my momma." The Chaplain of the hospital came in to see me. He was an Assemblies of God minister. God had sent him to me when I had no one else. He was supportive during this time and he encouraged me in the Lord and had prayer with me and with my momma. James came to see her. She loved him. He could make her mad sometimes, but James always thought my momma was a classy woman. She perked up for just a little bit. She knew he was there.

During one of the nights with my momma, I opened my Bible to the Book of Psalms, chapter 86. I was dealing with regret. Regret for not spending time in prayer with momma, reading the Bible with her, or just laying with her. I was wondering what had transpired in her heart since I prayed the sinner's prayer with her one year ago. I don't rely heavily on the method of just opening the Bible to a random passage but what I read was comforting to me. Psalm 86:13, "For great is Your mercy and loving kindness toward me: and you have delivered me from the depths of Sheol." You see I had been so busy trying to meet the physical demands and needs of my parents, trying to be a new mom that I didn't have time to foster and cultivate spiritual seeds for my momma. I was so concerned. My momma went into the hospital on a Friday. Sunday morning when my daddy was leaving the hospital and I was making my way there, my mother died alone with no one at her side. I did not have a lot of regrets up to that point because my life was dedicated to meeting their needs, but it hurts terribly that I did not make it to the hospital in time to be there with her in her last minutes. I couldn't imagine my momma whom I loved so very much dying alone, and those thoughts of her being alone cause great pain.

I was left to help my daddy deal with the tragedy of losing the love of his life after 32 years. Momma was only 48 years old. James did not know what to do. He didn't know how to handle such grief again. He closed himself up in the living room, as a way of escape to deal with things his own way. The grief he gave me was overwhelming when I needed him desperately. Thankfully he was able to compose himself to go to my momma's funeral. He loved momma and I knew momma had a special place in her heart for him. I knew he was having a hard time dealing with yet another tragedy. We really hadn't had much time for ourselves at this point in our marriage. I was so busy taking care of everyone else.

CHAPTER TEN

Shortly after the funeral, there was someone from the postal service that knocked on the door for a special delivery. It was the acceptance letter into the 2003 nursing school program that I needed to send to Raleigh (just in time for the requested deadline). School kept me busy, along with being mommy to precious Kayla and trying to help my daddy through the grieving process. I stayed so busy I didn't have time to grieve myself. Again, this was a coping mechanism that kept me in survival mode. There were some situations that arose that made me cry and some that made me pray and seek God. Daddy went to church some and said he liked the preacher. He agreed to let me pay tithes out of his finances. My Aunt Barbara recently told me how daddy's eyes got big when I told him how much I was giving in tithe money, but he still let me pay tithes.

Daddy was in desperate need to be on disability. I would continue to help him on the paper route and see him literally fall to the ground where his legs would give out on him. I knew he was not going to be able to keep lifting and bending like he had been. I finally convinced daddy to consider quitting the route and apply for disability. He had a little money from an insurance policy that could possibly carry him through. My daddy was frugal. He would get so tickled when James would stop by and take him something to eat.

Daddy would come over when he was able and would help watch Kayla if something came up. I had no time to cultivate friendships, and seemed to drift away from those I had, except for my mother-in-law. I was still trying to help her as much as I could too. She had helped us watch Kayla quite a bit. She started having chest pains. I told James I didn't want anything to happen to mom. We ended up putting Kayla in a nursery close to where

James worked. I cried and cried. I didn't like it. One day mom watched her and said Kayla went to stand in the corner and said she was not going back to that place. Who in the world would put a sweet 17-month old toddler who didn't bite or hit in a corner? I was furious. We were able to get her into a 5-star school. It still broke my heart to have to leave her crying. I believe God gave me this precious gift to raise myself, not so I can pay someone else to share the privilege given to me to nurture her. Fortunately, I got a grant where child care was paid for while I was in school. It was not easy. I believe she had 15 incident reports where she had been bitten by other children.

As far as my marriage I felt if we could make it through nursing school, we would survive. James expected me to be all and do all, but I could only do so much. I had to study. I did not have a brilliant mind. Kayla was a toddler and my daddy needed my help. I know it was hard for James after working all day and tending to her needs at night. The house was a disaster which always flipped switches for him but having a nursing degree would be what would get us through some really tough times that we were going to face financially.

I did rotations at Broughton Hospital, the mental institution we have nearby, during my psychiatric nursing classes. I had very few encounters with the mentally ill in my life. At least that is what I thought. After obtaining some knowledge, I found myself diagnosing people all the time. As a charismatic believer, I had a closed mind to believe that those with mental illness were demon possessed. I was very familiar with the story of the Maniac of Gadara, where a man was chained, naked, and filled with thousands of demons. I have been in a few church services where demons have manifested and I witnessed the delivering hand of God. As Christians, I do not believe we have a grip on mental illness nor how to help people who suffer from it. My eyes were enlightened to how widespread and common mental illness truly is. I left clinicals crying almost every day. It was so overwhelming. I see mental illness in unprecedented numbers. A lot of our homeless population suffer from mental illness because the government has done away with so many programs that would afford them the help they need.

PERSONAL INSIGHT

Do I believe some people are possessed? I most definitely without a doubt believe there are people walking around possessed by the devil. We can invite spiritual darkness into our lives just like we can invite the light. But there are those who literally suffer from chemical imbalances and disorders such as Bipolar disorder, Schizophrenia, personality disorders (I feel this one borderlines possession), depression and the list goes on and on. It is not their fault. I read reports all the time of how so many attempt suicide. I remember caring for a patient when I worked in the hospital who had come in for various reasons but had attempted several times to take his life. It was heartbreaking to hear that he had eventually succeeded. It is a demonic spirit that tries to cause God's children to take their lives because Satan can't stand us. He wants us dead. We look just like God; we were created in His image and he will do everything he can to try to wipe us out and separate us from God forever. There is a difference between depression and oppression. I know what it's like to experience both. There is a heaviness that you can't explain. The spirit of suicide came against me before I gave my heart to Jesus and even afterwards. It is horrible. I had enough Jesus to rebuke the enemy and plead the blood of Jesus over my life. Listen, if you have thoughts of harming yourself or others, call 911. Get help, but please don't wait until you get to this point. Seek counsel when you start noticing signs of depression. I prefer to have hands laid on me by God fearing believers, full of the Holy

Ghost who know how to pray. There is power in prayer, but I also believe God has given the medical profession knowledge to help in these areas even if for short-term treatment.

I had a Christian doctor tell me after all the tragedies I had experienced that serotonin levels were really low in my brain, and that I needed something to help with that. She loved God, and I trusted her but I didn't want to be dependent on a medication to see me through. She explained that it could take 5 years for someone to recover from one tragedy, but I had experienced several. There were more to come; you will hear about the others soon. With her godly counsel, I decided to try treatment. I tried at least 3 or 4 different classes of anti-depressants to find that I could not tolerate any of them. If you are one of these individuals like myself who are sensitive to medications, then we must hold on tight to the hand of God. Get in His presence and dwell there. There have been studies to show there is literally a change that occurs in the brain when someone is spending time in worship and praying in tongues as I referred to earlier in this book.[5]   This is how I have survived. This has been my Divine therapy. Understand that there is a place for medicine.   I do not condemn or judge anyone who takes anti-depressants and neither should you. Just know there are side effects, and you must follow up appropriately with your physician and be monitored. Just be proactive and stay on top of things. Don't allow the medicine to change who you are and find someone who you will allow to hold you accountable. You should not be "out of your mind" or lethargic. This is not what the medication is used for. Know that God wants you to rely on Him, and trust Him through the difficult days. You will be ok.

———————————————

[5] Carey, B. (2006, November 7). *A Neuroscientific Look at Speaking in Tongues.* Retrieved from http://www.nytimes.com/2006/11/07/health/07brain.htm l

It was so ironic and amazing how God puts all the pieces together in our lives. I stopped by my daddy's after class one day surprised to see this beautiful older lady sitting on his couch, rolling up coins. My Aunt Judy was there and she asked her, "Momma, do you know who this is?" "Yes, she said, "That is Diane." I wanted to cry. I recall how we would stop by her house every once in a blue moon and how she would run to the bedroom and slam the door. I remember her peeking out the door as if she was afraid. I don't know how my daddy was raised and what all he and his siblings endured. Some have said my grandmother was kept a prisoner. I don't know. Aunt Judy took grandma to the doctor after my grandpa died. He passed away shortly after Robert drowned and my momma's sister died 2 months before Robert's death. There has to come a time when we come to terms with our past and to receive God's forgiveness, we have to forgive. Mark 11:26 (NASB) states, "But if you do not forgive, neither will your Father who is in heaven forgive your transgressions."

I remember daddy going to see his dad at the hospital. Someone told me he had given his heart to God. That was a relief. But isn't it sad that my grandparents, my parents, maybe your family and friends live an entire life without knowing the goodness of God? Without knowing His love and knowing how to truly love others? If one could just taste of His goodness, how can you want or long for anything else? He fulfills every void and every longing in the soul. My grandmother was diagnosed with Schizophrenia. She lived her entire life in a mental prison when all she needed was some medication to stabilize the imbalances in her brain. How heart wrenching is this? I was so saddened by the thoughts that an entire generation could have been changed if she could have lived a normal life. This would not have fixed the way my grandpa treated her or his children. But what if someone would have told them about Jesus much sooner? Are you and I the missing link to bring HOPE to the lost and help change the course for future generations? It's not about me. It's not about you. It's about HIM. It's about rescuing lives from a burning hell where people will spend eternity. Doesn't that make us want to do something? We need to step out of our comfort zone and share the love of God with the hurting, the dying, and the lost.

CHAPTER ELEVEN

I survived nursing school; my daddy and Geneva (who I call mom) came to my pinning ceremony. My daddy was so proud. He could not believe that I was getting a nursing degree. I was a little frustrated...well maybe a lot...because I was graduating with Honors and that was not recognized at the ceremony that night. I realized that was a small thing, but nursing school was horrible and not an easy feat, and to graduate with Honors was a great accomplishment. I was so disappointed that daddy didn't get to see the recognition that night. I spoke with individuals at the school to find that it was an error. I wanted to make daddy so proud.

After graduating nursing school, I started my career at a hospital in 2005. I wrote a letter to Kayla while I was in school, and I told her how I wanted to find a weekend job, so I could be with her through the week and wouldn't have to leave her. I was blessed to work Friday and Saturday nights for 18 months. It was such a great hospital with phenomenal mentors and mentor programs. I wanted to go to critical care unit but was scared. I felt like I had mastered the orthopedic/neurology floor and felt I was ready for a change. I went through a critical care 8-week training and had the chance to go to CCU but turned down the opportunity because of fear. I ran myself to pieces on the progressive coronary floor. I knew if I didn't get off that floor, I was going to have a heart attack myself.

Shortly after completing my training on my husband's birthday, mom, my best friend died. She was placed in a facility for rehab after she had suffered a stroke. The facility did not monitor her blood work appropriately and she ended up with an intracranial bleed. I miss Geneva. She was not only the greatest mother-in-law in the world, but she was my best friend of 13 years.

I miss our time together, our talks, and our prayers. She made biscuits once for me to sell, so I could raise money to go with the youth to the yearly youth conference. She loved me like I was her daughter. I used to cut her hair. I would buy her dresses and they would fit her perfectly. She wouldn't even have to go out. I used to take her to pay her bills, until I convinced her she could trust the mail delivery system and send payments through the mail. I remember taking her and Angie to Alabama when her mother passed away. We would have Thanksgiving together. She would spend Christmas nights with us.

More than anything I missed the prayers she would pray for us. I knew she would lay in bed and intercede for me and James, and all her children and grandchildren. She loved God with all her heart. I recall dropping her off at home after a Sunday night service. She wanted to receive the Baptism of the Holy Spirit. She was in the spirit of worship and I laid hands on her that night in her driveway and she received the gift. I would go to her house to stay during fasts. I did not get to spend much time with her during the last year prior to her death because of the new job and all the other things I had on my plate. For that I am so ashamed.

James struggled through another year of dealing with pain and regret. He became angrier because of all the things that transpired up until the time of her death. I encouraged James to walk in forgiveness but I knew he could not do it without the help of the Holy Spirit. As a result of all the emotions and raw feelings, he did not see his baby sister, Angie, who had Down's syndrome until her death. She loved her family and all she ever wanted was for everyone to come see her and spend time with her.

Angie was so special. She loved presents of all sorts, particularly coloring books and Pringles. She loved television but most of all she loved her family. She would say, "Come here brother. Come here ayla. Come here Iana." She would ask, "What do you have for me?" She loved Kayla and would be so upset if she missed coming over a day. She would get upset during Kayla's toddler years because Kayla wanted to watch the Wiggles over and over and Angie got sick of seeing the Wiggles wiggle, but mom would always let Kayla watch them. Bless her heart. Angie loved God. She loved to worship. She loved Brother Miles and Tyron, the music director. Her favorite song was "I'll Fly Away". When the church would sing that song, I literally thought we were going to fly away. The glory of God would fall on that precious angel. I don't have a whole lot of major regrets, but missing out on time with her will always bother me. I let mom down. I let Angie down. Angie was diagnosed with bone cancer. God's grace and loving hand was on that baby as He was preparing her to meet Him. What potentially could have been a long, drawn-out, painful disease was reduced significantly. He did not allow Angie to suffer long or hard from my understanding. Angie passed away in January 2015, nine years after mom's passing. I long for the day when I can see her whole. I can see her standing in front of the choirs in heaven singing with all her might, with the most beautiful voice with her hands raised praising Jesus as her mom dances and rejoices with her. Jim Hill wrote, "What a day that will be when my Jesus I shall see, when I look upon His face, the One Who saved me by His Grace."

James wished he would have done something different. We all do. I can only imagine how disappointed mom would have been had she seen all that transpired. I am ashamed of my own attitude and behaviors and have found myself asking mom to please forgive me. I never wanted to hurt her in any way. I was heading out to visit my best friend in Virginia when I spoke with Angie for the first time in years. She wanted a SpongeBob watch. That was the first thing I tried to find when I got to Virginia. I did not realize she was going to pass away so quickly. God showed her mercy by allowing her to pass so quickly after diagnosis so she would not have to suffer.

I know James would do some things different if he had the chance. God is the healer of our wounds. I have seen God do an amazing job in helping James forgive, an answer to a prayer of mine for many years. We cannot help when other people do not forgive, but we are required to walk in forgiveness if we want the favor of God on our life. We can only pray that the same Spirit that deals with our hearts will also deal with theirs. Does forgiveness mean you must speak to someone or be their best friend? I'm not sure that it does. Is this possible? Yes, all things are possible with God. God is the restorer of our souls and He can restore any broken relationship. I have seen Him do that in so many ways.

CHAPTER TWELVE

I made a decision to find a job closer to home in March of 2007 and found myself trying to enter into a different kind of nursing: home health. It was rather interesting because the scope of nursing is broad. There is so much that a home health nurse can do and it involves a lot of hands-on nursing. My supervisors were Melanie Fox and Tonya Chester. The Lord used them in many ways during difficult times through many seasons of my life. I had the privilege of working alongside Melanie in two different roles for seven years. I had the opportunity to train nurses in different settings which led me to work in a fairly new type of nursing, which I love. Bosses and supervisors, you can make a difference in your employee's lives. Believe in them, have compassion, and empathy for them. It's amazing how you can bless others in this role.

Easter Sunday came and James asked me if I was going to cook something to eat for daddy. I had taken Kayla to have Easter pictures made. I made daddy pork chops and angel eggs (no room for deviled eggs in my home). I had seen daddy Saturday when I stopped by. He was in an unusual amount of pain and said to me, "Sister, I wished you would have brought me some bread. My legs hurt so bad." I went to the store and picked up a few things for him to eat. On Sunday, I asked daddy if he thought he could watch Kayla for a little while Thursday. The Lord had always provided a way when we needed help with Kayla. Some opportunities were not from Him, but we were so blessed when God moved our neighbors Chelsea and Mike beside of us. Chelsea was a Godsend and was always willing to assist in not just watching Kayla, but getting her places. She has recently endured the tragic death of her brother and the loss of her grandmother. I continue to keep her in my prayers. Chelsea will never know how much she means to me. I hope she can one day. We are blessed to be surrounded by wonderful neighbors. Sarah is a grandmother figure to Kayla. She has welcomed her over for ice cream sandwiches and sweet tea and bakes Kayla zucchini bread. I'm so thankful for the love she has shown her.

James and I had plans to attend a dinner at the church. We had not been alone since we had our Kayla-bug. She had just turned 5 years old in February. I was in training, so I didn't get to see daddy every day. I was not used to working full-time. My hours would eventually be full-time weekend hours but my training was during the week. I tried to call daddy Tuesday but could not get him to answer. I tried calling him again on Wednesday but was not able to reach him and he hadn't called me back. Thursday came. I called and left several messages. I received a call, "He has been sleeping all day." My heart began to race. "I don't think he is breathing." I called 911 as I got into my car. I couldn't get there quick enough. I was still on the phone with the operator when I arrived. Daddy was laying across the bed with his head on his arm. I rolled him over and rigor mortis had already begun setting in. There's no telling how long he had been laying there unresponsive. I didn't care that I was a nurse. I couldn't think straight. I was angry…I had never screamed like I screamed that day out of anger and disbelief. The male asked me, "Ma'am can you get him on the floor?" Totally out of character for me, I yelled at the individual who had been there cleaning all day, "You know daddy snores, why didn't you check on him?" By that time the paramedics had arrived, my daddy was dead, but because of my hysterics and their compassion they worked him up like they would anyone. They stuck an IV in him, hooked him up, and with all the hope and wishful thinking I had, I didn't want to believe he was gone.

I called James who was at the ballfield with Kayla and told him just to stay there because she did not need to see this. I told him, "He's dead." God in His grace had sent my cousin down the street at the exact time the ambulance was there. She came in and just held me. She had been to church with me several times before. She had given her heart to Jesus. I prayed in the Holy Ghost. I didn't know what else to do.

Theresa has a powerful testimony of her own. She lived with us on and off as a child and teenager. I did not know what all she had gone through. She is so beautiful and I wanted to be like her growing up. I remember being bold and telling my momma she loved Theresa more than she loved me. I also remember the sting of her hand as it went across my face. Momma knew what Theresa had gone through and she just wanted to be there for her. She loved her like she was her own child. Theresa drove me to the hospital and back home. I asked my aunt if there was anything my daddy had said. She said the night before he had prayed and told God if he was going to hurt like this the rest of his life to please let him die. I have struggled with where my daddy may be today. I have cried and cried but have come to the place where I just have to rely on the *Rhema* Word that God gave me in my early walk with him.

The officer that worked the scene called me later that night...or I may have called her, because daddy had medicine that I didn't want anyone to get a hold of. She had told me that someone had stolen my dad's pain medicines a few weeks ago and she had gone out to get a report. Daddy told James about this but with our busy schedules he did not think to mention it to me. This is why daddy was in so much pain when I saw him that Saturday. He had been without pain medicine for 2 weeks. He was on Methadone for his chronic pain. Daddy was a smart man. He was frugal with his medicine and would take ½ tablets instead of whole tablets. Some family members were coming in and out and had stolen the medicine.

BUT the officer told me that I was all that daddy could talk about that night and how proud he was of me. He never came out and told me in his own words, but he was bragging to others about me. She just wanted to let me know how much he loved me. I listened to the answering machine and my Aunt Barbara's voice was on there, "Top of the morning." She and daddy always said that to each other. "Ricky pick up," she would say. She loved my daddy so much. I had to call her and let her know she wouldn't get to hear his voice again. Momma and Daddy named me after her. She was called Diane, but has recently taken on her first name to try to remove the painful memories of her past. She lives in Georgia. I hope she knows how much I love her and how much I appreciate the love she has shown to Kayla. I am proud of all she has overcome in her life and the love she has for our Lord and Savior. She has experienced many tragedies including an extremely painful childhood. You would never know it. I hope one day she will be able to share her testimony with me. I'm encouraging her to write her story to tell the world how God rescued her.

Aunt Barbara and I were communicating recently while I was editing this book. She told me, "I have learned a lot since Ricky died. He loved Jesus and when we were delivering papers we would say, 'I can do all things through Christ which strengthens me.' I've learned we can't earn our righteousness; it is a free gift from God. We just have to believe Romans 10:9-10 and Ricky did. He trusted Jesus to get him through each day. I know he will be there to say 'top of the morning' to us when we get to heaven."

There was an autopsy completed on my daddy. His body looked horrible, as you could see the staples in his head from where they cut him open. I thought it took an awfully long time to get the results. I had to call the state numerous times and they had no record of having his blood sample. I had to call and follow up with the city. They always take 2 samples just in case something like this happens and, believe me, if it could happen it did, and has happened to me countless times. It is draining and overwhelming that someone can be the victim of so many people's mistakes. Still to this day, I feel like I have to spin my wheels because people don't do their jobs right, and I have to spend precious time and energy trying to fix it. This absolutely drains me. This can't be normal?

Daddy had a little money in the bank. I took it and deposited it to pay for his funeral. The bank attendant had been on the phone with someone. I had written the check to the funeral home and it bounced. After researching, crying, and praying, we discovered that the attendant had deposited it the wrong person's account and they had already spent all the money.

The bank assured me the deposit was insured and they were able to work out the details.

The report finally came showing a Methadone overdose. I 100% believe and know that my daddy would not ever try to take his own life. I had given him scriptures in the past and talked to daddy about how we do not have the right to take our own life and that only God has that right. 1Corinthians 3:17 tells us if we defile or destroy our temple, then God will destroy us. I do believe that he took his usual dosage (however much that was) but you can't do that with Methadone. It must be titrated up slowly. The individual who stole his medicine was to blame from my perspective.

Three days after my daddy's death, he received a check in the mail for his disability, going back to cover when he first filed. The total of that check was $30,000. He knew he was going to get this money, and I know my daddy was waiting for it. I knew my daddy too well. I remember writing our Congressman for daddy and taking him to the courthouse to pursue disability for him. Just like I told the judge when my mom was turned down, does someone who really deserves assistance have to be almost dead? This is really tough for me to handle when so many abuse this area.

PERSONAL INSIGHT

My parents never intended to become dependent on pain medicine. They were hard-working, normal people and their physically hard labor had caused wear and tear on their bodies. At this time there wasn't a lot of control with narcotics in the healthcare system. The government has since heavily regulated this. Because of people who have abused the system, individuals are stereotyped who take pain medicine. As for myself I have a personal commitment to not use narcotics, and pray I can manage the pain I have with natural resources. I have quickly stopped them after having surgeries. Unless you have endured or experienced the pain that I've seen or felt, you cannot begin to know what it is like to live with chronic pain. Yes, we must have regulations. Yes, pain medicine is addictive, and I would like to see it used as sparingly as possible. I also understand how hard it is to live without some type of relief. I utilize chiropractic care, ice and heat, and pray this will be all I ever need. I thank God for my chiropractor. My parents were unfortunate that they had ruptured discs and back surgeries. It would have helped if they could have quit their jobs and not kept reinjuring themselves. For most people that isn't possible and especially wasn't for my parents. You must depend on the Lord and you have to be determined that you will not allow yourself to become addicted to these medications.

If I ever felt an attack of the enemy against my home, this was definitely the time. With losing daddy: I was left trying to care for my aunt, trying to be a mom while working full-time, all while my husband was put on the back burner again. My brother told me I could do whatever I wanted to do with the house, so I allowed my aunt to stay there as long as she needed. It is still unclear to me who stole my daddy's medicine, but it was someone in the family. There must be someone who will stand up and say....NO MORE!! I refuse for the generational curse to continue in my family. It is broken by the renewing power of Jesus Christ.

James's faith had been affected by this time on a pretty serious level. I didn't realize how close he had grown to my daddy. He had been stopping by to see him often. He was the closest thing to a father figure James had in a long time. Daddy called him Bubba. I was trying to learn a new job, take care of Kayla and was determined this time to stay active teaching the kiddos at church, all while having to deal with the human errors mentioned above and one of the most horrible experiences I had ever faced with someone I thought God had sent into my life to offer her friendship.

Did you know the Bible tells us if we hate a brother or sister it is murder. (1 John 3:15) Within one month of my father dying and carrying the weight I had on me, I found that lies had been told to someone very special to me; not only did she believe this individual, but someone I would have never thought did as well. I never want to hurt anyone. I knew they were lies; seven years later my friend contacted me and apologized as I was getting ready to leave for work. Messed my make-up all up. I've always been extremely tough on Kayla expecting her to be well-behaved. She pretty much has been the target of meanness in so many situations, but I still expect her to take the higher ground. Not only did I have to deal with this painful betrayal that centered around my daughter, but I noticed peculiar behaviors with my husband.

Yes, James and I have had hard times. We have struggled in our marriage. Who wouldn't under the circumstances we have been faced with, but James has always had a heart for God. He has been delivered from drugs and alcohol, and has not wanted any of that since he had been saved.

I woke up one night to loud noises outside. It was around 3 o'clock in the morning. I could hear James stuttering and talking to someone about God. I woke up the next morning to get ready to go to church and went outside to find broken beer bottles on our patio. My heart sank deep into the core of my body. I couldn't believe it. This went on for weeks. He had missed going to church at least 3 Sundays. I told him, "You better wake up. You are going to lose your wife and your daughter but most importantly you are risking going to hell. He was my daddy. You can't stop serving God." Who could I tell? I felt like I had absolutely no one, especially no one who would not judge my husband. Only

God, and friend I promise you He is all you really need, even when those you have considered your friends for more than a decade turn on you. I handled things like I had up to that point on my knees. No one but God could understand the absolute pain I was enduring.

I just wanted to die and there were times I asked God to please take me home but Kayla needed her momma and I couldn't let her down. This man was on my couch one Sunday morning. I have a heart of compassion for alcoholics and drug addicts, but I knew what the devil was doing and I wasn't putting up with it. I told him about Jesus, but I also told him he wasn't welcome in my home and to never come back. He used to work with James and admitted he "had seen a difference in him." He apologized and has not been back. I do pray that he finds peace with his soul.

I wished I could say I have done everything right and that I prayed enough, fasted enough, but I know in my heart I could have done more. On this path, I had gotten weary. I have gotten side-tracked many times. There were times I had sinned along the way, but I did not start this race to give up. God's word tells us that a righteous man falls seven times BUT HE GETS BACK UP (Proverbs 24:16)!!! I am not a quitter. The pain is still real and it hurts, but He is the Healer. I have not been to the grave site since I buried my daddy. There lies my brother, mother, father, grandmother, and my aunt. Maybe one day I can go.

CHAPTER THIRTEEN

In 2008, the following year on my way to taking Kayla to school, I was stopped at the red light in our neighborhood. The light turned green and I proceeded. As I looked to the left I saw a big Chevy truck going full speed as it rammed me right in my side. James' friend was working on my little Nissan and was supposed to have it back to me the night before so I could go to work. I was working out in the field doing home health. Something came up with the car and he told us he needed to keep it another day. I was in our SUV that morning. Had I been in the Nissan, I would have been killed. Everyone left the scene of the accident. Does anyone know what happens under these circumstances? I remember seeing a truck behind me. He drove off. It was 7:50 am. NO ONE STOPPED even though I had a little child. I called James and told him. He was just thinking about how much he loved us and felt something in his spirit. There were no broken bones, no blood but I was in quite a bit of pain, so much that I had to cut my hours back at work. The police officer declared no one to be at fault. The vehicle was almost new so it wasn't totaled. James had an idea to help find the person who hit us: put an ad in the local paper. We received a call from a dad, whose son had called him on the way to school. He had seen the accident and didn't know what to do. He had called the cops to report it but no one followed up. Thankfully this was the witness we needed to help us with expenses and medical bills.

I remember Kayla saying when she saw the damage to the SUV, "Daddy's going to be so mad momma; it's got a scratch." She knew how particular her daddy was but he was thankful that we were both alive and okay. It was during this time that an attack of fear came against me, not knowing when or if God would take my husband or Kayla away from me. It was frightening to me. The following fall, the coach of Kayla's Upward basketball team was the daddy who called us from the ad. How amazing and just like God to show up and show us that He cares about and orchestrates every detail in our lives!

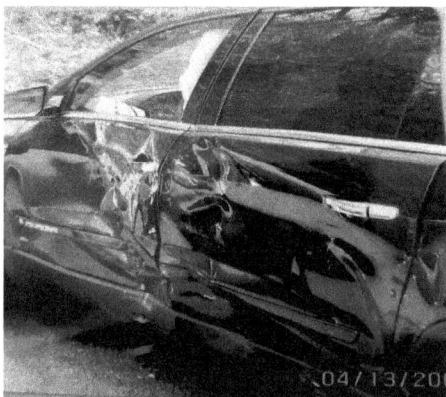

Kayla was dancing at this time. We met a family through dance that had become our best friends. Even during all the turmoil and pain, I was still trying to get others to go to church with me. The Chronister's eventually came. Angela was raised in the Church of God and she wanted to get back in church. It was uncanny how much we had in common. They delivered newspapers too. How crazy is that? For the first time, we had a family with whom we could do things together. We went to the mountains together and spent nights together. They were an answer to prayer in our lives, but God called them back to their home town in 2011. We were devastated but God had a plan for their lives. God blessed my best friend to be able to go to nursing school and better their situation. I do not like to travel. Once someone leaves or I move to another job or situation changes in my life those relationships pretty much dissipate. But I will pack up my car a few times a year to go spend time with some of the greatest people we know. I will be forever grateful to God for the Chronister family: Angela, David, Laken and Tinley. Angela's family, her mom, Faye, dad, Dave, her sister Jessica and aunt and uncle, Kat and Ron treat us like we are a part of their family. We were truly blessed the day our paths crossed at Krista Whitener's Academy of Dance.

We had been at a church for 8 years. I stayed faithful in teaching on Wednesday nights and helping with children's plays. Some things transpired that I could no longer support and I asked James to take me somewhere else. James overcame drinking a lot and got to where he would drink one at night because he couldn't sleep well. I didn't like it, but I loved him and I had to trust God on his behalf. He made the mistake of leaving a beer can at the couch one night and Kayla saw it. She cried so hard asking me, "Is daddy going to go to hell, mommy?" It is easy to justify things when we are partaking in certain things. The Bible says every man is right in his own eyes (Proverbs 21:2). I will not debate this topic in this book. What I do know is once God delivers you from something, He means for you not to pick it back up.

I visited a church in Newton on Mother's Day in 2011. I loved it, but wanted to go where I felt comfortable and had some friends. Kayla and I wanted to attend a church in Hildebran, but James wanted to go to a church in Newton. I acted unbecoming about things. While getting ready for church, the Holy Spirit stopped me and spoke to my heart and said, "You will go to church with your husband and you won't give him a hard time." I said, "Yes Sir." I could tell things were starting to affect him spiritually, and it was not worth seeing him decline even more. I went and woke hubby up and said, "Kayla and I are going with you to church." We started attending this church. The messages are powerful and the worship is phenomenal. The Holy Spirit has dealt with both of us during our time there.

It wasn't long after we started attending our new church that I began having major physical issues, yet another hindrance to me being able to commit to work in the church or build new relationships. The huge betrayal didn't help much either. I went years living in pain and having strange symptoms that weren't explainable and seeking treatment to be told nothing was wrong with me. Scans and diagnostic tests were fine. James and I were always able to work out our differences through intimacy and that had been majorly affected with the pain I endured. Ladies, the Bible tells us that our bodies are not our own; they belong to our husbands (1 Corinthians 7:4). I want to be a good and godly wife. God created men with certain desires. It is important to not say no!

In 2012, on my way home, minding my own business at a stop light a Hummer that looked like they were pulling over to the right lane, backed up and hit me with a hard impact totaling my Nissan (which was paid off). I am embarrassed to say during prayer that morning, I recall telling the Lord how "it would be nice to have a newer car." This wasn't exactly how I had anticipated that prayer being answered.

In 2013, I ended up in the ER with chest pain and shortness of breath from a medicine that I was taking to help with the painful symptoms I was having. It was a hormone that I had never taken before. Being proactive, I found a surgeon who was willing to do a hysterectomy. I can imagine what he thought when he saw the literal book I had written begging him to perform a hysterectomy. I was his last surgical patient before he retired and I remember him saying, "It's been a pleasure getting to take care of you." Oh, how I thank the Lord for Dr. Griffin! The inner layer of my uterus was filled with fibroids but weren't showing up on a CT scan. My ovaries were filled with cysts. I lived in pain for so long. I managed to get through work but missed out on so much with Kayla. Things had gotten really tough financially for us after the first accident. James and I were looking at losing everything we had. Kayla had been in a Christian school all her life. We were looking at having to enroll her in public school in the 3rd grade because of what we were facing. The headmaster of the school called me three times that summer. He told me Kayla was an asset and that he didn't want to see her go. The school blessed us that year and was an answer to many of our prayers for Kayla. I cried and thanked the Lord because I didn't want her to go to public school. James didn't either at this time in her life.

The Lord provided a new job opportunity for me closer to home in April of 2014. This year would prove to be yet another difficult year. I stopped at a gas station on my way to a lunch meeting. I wanted a donut so badly. That donut cost me a lot of time and money. That was an expensive donut! I just took my debit card in…when I came back out someone had crashed my window and had stolen my purse. Oh, the headache of losing cards and having to change bank accounts! I had that bank account since I was 17. My prayer was that whoever stole my purse would listen to the message I had in there from church and maybe one day it gets back to me that they repented and gave their heart to Jesus.

Later in the summer, lightning struck our house and hit our air unit. James was let go from his job and I started to have crazy symptoms: not being able to breathe and my shoulder blades hurting. My chest would hurt and I would get nauseated and sick to my stomach. Again, tests were done and nothing showed up. Insurance originally denied the request to have my gallbladder removed. I was not a textbook case. I wrote a letter and the surgeon called for a peer to peer discussion. The Lord blessed me again after being proactive. After having the gallbladder removed in March of 2015, I haven't had any of these symptoms since and I praise God for the sense He gives me and the endurance to not give up nor take no for an answer. I also had the second ovary removed during this surgery that was causing so much pain. This has been great but it opened a whole different can of worms dealing with hormones. I am thankful that my husband has been patient with me in this area. You post-menopausal and surgical menopausal women know what I am talking about. The struggle is real; there is different pain that affects intimacy. I have discovered that there is a procedure called the Mona Lisa that appears to be helpful to relieve post-menopausal pain.

James has had struggles with his jobs and those he has worked with. People were constantly trying to get to him. He was able to control his anger at work. After he would tell me some of the things people would say to him, I knew it was God that gave him the self-control he needed. He has been a hard worker for his family. He struggled with sleep as I mentioned before. The assisted living facility he worked for took advantage of him. He was on call 24-7 and he treated that place like his home and took such good care of it. They would call him at Kayla's birthday parties, when we were away, and during dance recitals. They ended up letting him go in 2014. This gave him a chance to have some time for himself. He has always worked hard for our family. It gave me a chance to focus on my new job and build a program without having to worry about picking Kayla up from school and making sure she was ok.

On March 3, 2015 James called me at work. He was on his way to a job interview and had a car accident two days before my surgery was scheduled. Someone pulled out in front of him, and it totaled the vehicle we almost had paid off. I was so concerned for the young lady and her daughter. I am so thankful that the Lord protected everyone and that no one was seriously injured that day. I still deal with pain from the accident in 2008 where I was T-boned the way this little car was. Later that summer, James was chopping a tree and a piece of metal shot into his leg. This was the year his baby sister passed away in January. He was feeling down because of losing his job but he was doing work on the side in HVAC; the Lord was providing for us.

PERSONAL INSIGHT

James has always been a giver. We both had been faithful in paying our tithes since we have been saved. I began applying this principle in my life immediately when I learned about it. I had never struggled with not paying our tithes until about a year or so ago. We had a discussion right before he had the accident and both agreed because of the situation we were in that we would not pay our tithes for a few months. I was pretty much always adamant and insisted that we always pay our tithes but said that, "Maybe the Lord would understand." We aren't saying that was the reason he had the accident but we both agreed it doesn't pay not to give God what belongs to Him. If you haven't been at a place to trust God in this area in your life, I urge you to walk in obedience and put this principle to practice in your life. We must be willing to let go of what most people count precious to them...money. God requires His children to give 10% of their earnings. Why? It costs money to share the gospel. The gospel is free but the light bill, buildings, and electricity are not. Malachi 3:8 (NIV) says, "Will a mere mortal rob God? Yet you rob me. But you ask, 'How are we robbing you?' In tithes and offerings." We are also mandated to honor our pastors and take care of them. "Charles Spurgeon once had the officers of a small country church ask him to recommend a pastor for them. But the salary they were prepared to pay was so small that he wrote back to them, 'The only individual I know, who could exist on such a stipend, is the angel Gabriel. He would need neither cash nor clothes; and he could come down from heaven every Sunday morning, and go back at night, so I advise you to invite him'"[6]

My heart is for missions and the work of God that literally transforms lives. I am limited in what I can do, because I must work. I also have physical limitations that

[6] Cole, S. J. (1994). "Lesson 17: Paying Your Pastor(s) (1 Timothy 5:17-18)". Retrieved from https://bible.org/book/export/html/21894

my life has brought upon me, but when I stand before God I want to be able to say I had a part in helping in missions by at least contributing to God-honoring honest ministries. I am careful where I put my money. I want to hear God's voice when it comes to giving and one day would like to be able to give tens of thousands of dollars to the work of the Lord.

Up to this point we have had some of the roughest and toughest years for two decades straight. My brother has been in car accidents, been homeless from a poor decision regarding daddy's house, and fell over from a heat stroke. As his praying sister I just kept pleading the blood over him and God has kept him alive. In 2015 he decided to try to learn how to drive a truck. He nearly gave up a few times; it was really scary for him and he would have panic attacks. The company that he started with had to be a Godsend because they actually cared for him. He was scared but I prayed that the Spirit of David would come over him and that God would give him courage. He called me one day when the news came out that same-sex marriage had been passed. Fear came over him and he realized all the things I had been sharing and sowing in his heart were coming to pass. He said that he didn't want to go to hell and that he wanted him and his fiancé to get married and serve God. HALLELUJAH TO THE LAMB OF GOD!!

He called me and told me he had a horrible dream on 1/28/16. He dreamed that he went to hell. He told me, "It looked like I saw the devil and they tied me up...and these beasts started to chew at me and eat my arms up." I asked him if he had made Jesus Lord of his life. I told him I had prayed many times that he would have dreams of hell and that he wouldn't want to go there. He said, "I woke up sweating." Again, I asked him if he had made Jesus Lord of his life. Something happened to the phone lines. We were still connected but I couldn't hear him. I told him to call me back, to pray, and ask the Lord to help him be strong. He had already asked Jesus into his heart previously but I know the flesh is weak and we must discipline it by surrendering to truth. James tells us that "the prayers of a righteous man or woman availeth much" (James 5:16). God's Word is true and He will keep His promises. My brother has been homeless many times. The struggles have been hard to bear knowing the conditions he has lived in. It wasn't too long ago that he just wanted to give up. He said, "I just couldn't get anything right." He told me he wanted to die and he meant it. I sensed the spirit of suicide strong over him. I cried out to God with all I had, and I interceded needing an answer quickly. I texted my aunt Barbara and asked her to agree with me. She is a prayer warrior and has faith. Ricky was in another state with no way to track him. God answered our prayers and God is blessing my brother. The Lord turned the situation around immediately. I can't thank God enough for taking care of him and bringing him out of the pit of despair and giving him hope again. I want to see him grow in the Lord to where he works to help others receive the truth that he has received. He watches our services online and I am working to encourage him to step out in faith and pay tithes. I believe he will. I love him so much. He will never know the tears I have cried and the prayers I have prayed for him until we make it home.

CHAPTER FOURTEEN

I was able to complete the majority of this book in January and was so excited that I could start encouraging and touching people's lives. This book is a perspective from just an everyday person trying to live out God's Word. I'm not in the "ministry" but what I do and what you do will speak volumes to people. This book is to encourage everyday people like you and I to know we can serve God with passion and touch individual lives with whom we are blessed to cross paths and that with Jesus we can weather the storms. What is the message we want to convey?

A few months have passed and I am now writing in October. I was not aware in January of what was getting ready to take place in my daughter's life. God doesn't allow us to see all the trials ahead of time before we go through them because I believe our hearts will become faint. He gives us strength during the storms. Kayla has given me permission to tell this story but before I share some of this with you, let me first tell you that this was an attack of the enemy against my daughter's faith, our home, and God's purpose in our lives. I can't say that I handled everything exactly the way I should have, but I tried. I struggled with faith during this time and looking back over the year, all I can say is God again confirms in my life that He really is who He says He is. I like the song by Natalie Grant that says, "How can I make you so small when You're the One who holds it all? How can I forget that You've always been the King of it all?" If you haven't heard that song, please take time to listen to the words.

I want you to understand that we can walk through these trials with confidence that God will bring us through to the other side. He is sharpening us, removing the things that don't belong, and refining us for greater things. We do not understand it at the time, and can't fully see until maybe years down the road. Every person of influence must have a wilderness experience. How we allow ourselves to bend will determine the length of our stay. Moses wandered for 40 years in the wilderness before God used him. Lord, please don't let it take me that long. Just understand before you read this that I am not mad at anyone but the devil. I see how he sets people up to try to destroy them, but I come against every wicked scheme of the enemy in your life and mine. He has no authority over God's children.

I have forgiven those who have caused great pain, but may not necessarily choose to allow them back in the same position they once held in my heart or life. Aren't you glad that no matter what we do, if we are truly sorry and repent, God will restore us to the exact position we had with Him and even higher. Again, we cannot be forgiven of our sins if we do not forgive or if we hold grudges. I have had some "Christians" talk to me in a way I would not speak to others. All we can do is pray for those who do not reflect Jesus and pray that the fruits of the Spirit will be manifested in their hearts. I do not want to be a person that someone says, "If that is what being a Christian is about, I don't want it." We need to think about our facial expressions, our body language, and our demeanor when we are at church and when we are in public. When visitors come to your church, do they see love? Do they see joy? OR do you walk right past someone and ignore them? I can't count the times I've smiled at known believers, said "hi" and they just walk away. Really? Everyone has trials, everyone has struggles but for the most part many would never know what I have gone through. We must make a conscious effort to portray the love of our Father. My daughter will make comments like, "I'm tired of smiling at people and they not smile back." My comment back to her is smile anyway. You are not responsible for others, but you are held accountable for your actions. If we will honor God and pray we will see God do more than we could ever do on our own. I have learned this the hard way.

During this time, I was inundated with thoughts like "What is the use? How can you help anyone if you can't help your own daughter? You're just a nobody!" During this trial, I literally felt like I was going to break, but I am a living testimony of His abounding grace. Kayla began having physical issues that tried to bring fear in my heart. She fell and hit her head pretty hard on Christmas day. She started having heart palpitations after coming back home from Karen Wheaton's Ramp and severe joint paint that scared all of us. We found out she had several deficiencies. I am so thankful for the knowledge God has given doctors.

Kayla told me this year she felt like, for the first time, that she had "true friends." We held a birthday party for her which had been so much fun. The following Monday something shifted and it would send Kayla on a downward spiral.

She found herself eating lunch with a favorite teacher for weeks. Kayla's demeanor changed and her countenance changed. My heart became heavier than ever. The "friends" would taunt her, make fun of her, and laugh at her. She had gained strength to walk by and say, "Hi guys," and just keep walking. The losses in her life and the feelings that no one could love her were all too overwhelming. The way her dad would get angry with her and the way things transpired with her friends had caused her to believe that God did not love her and that He was a mean God, which literally broke my heart.

Father, I pray for all the girls and guys who have been bullied or are currently being bullied. I ask that you would cover their minds. Instill within them their purpose. Let them see themselves as You see them. I pray for the confidence of the Holy Spirit to flood their souls. This too will pass. I pray for those who are mean spirited, who do not have a relationship with you. Those who try to work friends against each other. I pray for conviction of the Holy Spirit to flood their souls that they would see through Your eyes to have compassion and love for all your people in Jesus name.

This was a spiritual attack against my daughter, and I was so wrapped up in the emotions that I could not see clearly at times. God put in my spirit to get her out of the situation. He strategically opened doors so that she could finish the year through homeschooling. What a divine intervention!! This was huge to me, but unfortunately another problem was that much of this infiltrated into all of her other relationships advertently and inadvertently. She had given up and lost trust in everyone at this point.

Along with Kayla, I pulled myself away from the few friendships I had formed. She received a text from someone she held dear to her heart that said, "No wonder everyone hates you." I was taken off guard and couldn't imagine someone saying that to her. Kayla cried, as it broke her heart and just added to the thoughts that she was unlovable. When you begin to believe these lies, one starts to act out certain behaviors. I was in for a rough year, and all I had was hope that God would pull us through as He had so many times before.

Things like this happen all of the time, but we cannot allow it to cause dissention in our lives. If you cannot work through conflict with the individual, you should not go around discussing things with others to cause their opinions to be persuaded of them. This is called gossip, and I instructed Kayla through all of this not to discuss anything with anyone. I doubt she passed the test, because she's 14 and she had a lot of anger in her. Prayerfully, I can engrain this in her before she leaves from under our covering. I have been on both ends of this sinful act and I as I grow in Him, I prefer to stay away from it. I have been through too much to get entangled in such nonsense, and I hope I made at least a B+ with this test and can pass any future tests that may come my way. I pray for the spirit of discernment to detect this in others. When it comes to teenage girls I am the first to know that my daughter is not perfect and can be "ungodly" in her behavior at times. If she does something I want to know, because she will be corrected. Who do we think we are to believe none of us have sin in our hearts? That is the very reason Jesus suffered on the cross and to think we or our children have no sin would mean that His death was in vain.

PERSONAL INSIGHT

One area of growth I would like to see in the body of Christ and in my own life is how we handle conflict. I have talked to Kayla on several occasions about communicating with her friends and letting them know when something bothers her. Talk about it and move on. If they are true friends they will rise above. Don't hold things in, because it can cause feelings of bitterness and anger. The Bible gives us a correct way to deal with conflict. Listen, God will not receive our offerings of praise until we have first attempted reconciliation. The Bible says, "Leave your gift there in front of the altar. First go and be reconciled to them; then come and offer your gift" (Matthew 5:24). But if the friend is not willing to hear you out, the Bible tells us to take it to another step that most are not willing to do because of spiritual immaturity and/or fear of retaliation or rejection. "If your brother sins against you, go and tell him his fault, between you and him alone. If he listens to you, you have gained your brother" (Matthew 18:15, EVS).

According to Matthew 18:15-20, if a professed Christian is wronged by another, he shouldn't complain of it to others, which is what most do, but he should go to the offender privately, state the matter with kindness, and show him his wrongdoing. "This would generally have all the desired effect with a true Christian, and the parties would be reconciled. The principles of these rules may be practiced everywhere, and under all circumstances, though they are too much neglected by all. But how few try the method which Christ has expressly enjoined to all his disciples! In all our proceedings we should seek direction in prayer; we cannot too highly prize the promises of God. Wherever and whenever we meet in the name of Christ, we should consider him as present in the midst of us."[7] If going to the person does not resolve the issue, the Bible tells us to take someone with you: "But if they will not listen, take one or two others along, so that every matter may be established by the testimony of two or three witnesses" (Matthew 18:16, NIV). I have really tried hard to put into practice this command of God, and go to those who I've had an

---

[7] Henry, M. (1706). "The removal of offences." In *Matthew Henry's Concise Commentary on the Bible* (Retriieved online at http://www.ccel.org/ccel/henry/mhcc.xxxii.xviii.html). Grand Rapids, MI: Zondervan.

offense with or vice versa. It is not easy to do. A lot of times if they have proven to have a difficult spirit, I will just give them over to God. There are those I know who love God, and I know in time healing will take place. You have to pray to present things in a Godly manner. It is never good to say "you" when addressing an issue, but come through with the perspective, "I feel this way." This takes the sting of blame away from the individual you are trying to make amends with, making it much easier for reconciliation. I believe when we perfect this in our lives, we will have so much more power that the Lord said we would have. I will not be deterred by this, and I will continue to allow God to help me in this area. Will you?

Getting back to the story...Another friend of Kayla had her friend send a text to Kayla. I had a knee jerk reaction, because it was a threat sent to my daughter. I called this individual and told her she better never text my daughter again, or I would call the police. I monitor Kayla's text, her social media, and God has blessed me by using others to catch things that I miss. We have had heated discussions (that's what I call our fights) about what is appropriate and what is not appropriate to put on social media. I expect my child to act appropriately regardless, and I appreciate those who love us enough to keep me informed on things I may miss. Honestly friends, I became bitter and weary during this time. I was again reminded of the story of Ruth, particularly Naomi, where her husband and sons had gone to the land of Moab during a drought, where they were commanded not to go resulting in her loss of them. She said don't call me Naomi but call me Mara which means bitter. I told God, "I feel like I am bitter, and I don't want to be, God." His Holy Spirit has reminded me for every Naomi experience, there will come a time of redemption. We will recover all.

Kayla would see posts where other kids would be invited to events and she wouldn't receive an invitation, although she had regressed away from everyone, it was still painful. She took on the "I don't care attitude" which is a destructive way of dealing with pain. This is where social media can be dangerous, especially to teenagers who do not know where their identity lies. If you have a young child, I would seriously pray and think twice about allowing them to have a smartphone. I spent hours upon hours pouring into her. I have spoken life into her and declared that she has been created to change the world for God. I've instructed her that what she makes happens for others, God will make happen for her; the mercy we extend to others, will be the measure He extends to us. I've asked her to invest into girl's lives who feel alone and empty. When we serve we get our minds off of ourselves.

The enemy wants her to believe nothing works, but he is a liar. God loves

Kayla, He loves my husband, and, my friend, He loves you! I'm trusting He will help her with her trust issues. I believe He will also help her understand that He is our best friend and that our identity lies therein. I've taught her to pray for those that mistreat us. The Bible teaches us to love those that hate us (Matthew 5: 44). But I tell you, love your enemies and pray for those who persecute you. I must believe that the truths that I have instilled within her will follow her all the days of her life; that the Word will not return void and God will complete the work He has begun in her. I have also recently told her, "You will not allow your circumstances to dictate your behaviors. I have lost a lot in my life, but I have never missed work but maybe once or twice with permission. I did not miss school. You will do what you need to do, because life goes on, and you have to move forward. You will not have a victim mentality." This has been true in my life, and it is by God's strength and grace alone, that I have been able to be a productive, valued employee. He gets all the glory for the good in my life, and I am responsible for how I respond to the bad.

Kayla wrote a heartfelt letter and poem for my 44th birthday. I'd like to share the poem that I woke up to that morning:

The smiles, the laughs, and the love we share,

Nothing else in the world can compare.

The care you give, the love you show,

The lessons you teach me as I grow.

The words you comfort me with when I live in fear,

The happy times you've given me over the years.

The things you do, the things you say,

The nights we have laughed and the nights we have prayed.

For all of this I am extremely thankful,

To have a mother by my side through all the life events that are painful.

From night to night, from day to day,

I love you with all my heart and I'm happy to say..... Happy Birthday!!

I was able to take my birthday off with pay. I spent time cleaning the house and spent time in prayer. It was towards the end of praying that I received a text from Kayla that said, "If anything happens momma know that I love you and Happy Birthday. There is a lockdown and something about a shooter. IDK. It's real momma. Please pray."

I was at the school in no time and found myself across the street on my knees crying out to God. I asked another mom if she was a believer, and if she believed in prayer. We both declared no person or child would be harmed. They were on lockdown for hours. Police officers, troopers, and the SWAT team were all on the scene. It kind of put things in perspective quickly. Some say it was a hoax but regardless, I thank God in heaven above because, the greatest gift that day was that I got to hold my baby girl in my arms. Don't take life for granted friends. Embrace those God has given you and reach out to those who are lonely. I found out later that it bothered Kayla tremendously that only one person reached out to her that day to find out how she was doing. I encouraged her and told her several were texting me to check on her, but again this is a tactic of the enemy to try to get her to feel that no one cares about her. I renounce and come against his schemes because they will not work. I have since given her number to a handful of individuals that I know love her, so they can just pour into her when they feel led.

I'd like to request something of all of the prayer warriors reading this book. My heart is for the lost. I love people and I want God to use me to direct many to Him but in doing so, I don't want to lose my daughter. I believe as I walk in obedience, God will hear my heart's cry for my daughter.

I would ask that when you pray, please remember us, particularly my daughter. I believe she was created for greatness, to walk out the calling God has given her. There has been so much pain in her life that it has skewed her vision of God and His people. God wants to take pain and use it for purpose in her life, my life, and in your life. I believe God can and will use the younger generation to carry a Joshua anointing, and I believe God will use Kayla in ways I could only dream of for myself. Pray for protection over her heart, her mind, and her spirit. Pray that God will surround her with those who love her for who she is and who have her best interest at heart. Pray for a God-fearing man one day who will be gentle towards her in spite of her flaws. I believe you should pray these things over your children as well. Let's agree that our children will run after God with all their being.

I am hopeful that through counseling we can work to become a stronger family. I am excited and hopeful that we can work through some of the baggage that we have been carrying. I am asking God to continue to work on each of us and give hope to our daughter that He, indeed, uses different methods to help us get to where we need to be. He loves us individually and as a family unit and friend, He loves you.

CHAPTER FIFTEEN

As I have reflected on my life, it is evident how God has given me the grace to get through every situation I've faced, just like He will give you the grace to overcome the trials, the pain and the tragedies in your life. Have I prayed and wished things could be easy? You better believe it. That's a BIG YES!! Do I think I will never have any more trouble? It would be nice, but it isn't reality because it's through trials that integrity and character are built and I don't feel I am anywhere near where God is trying to get me to be. I'm declaring God's promises over me and my family along the way. Fear has tried to grip my heart many times but Isaiah 26:3 (NIV) says, "You will keep in perfect peace those whose minds are steadfast, because they trust in you." The devil hates us. We were created in the image of God and he gets really mad when we act like God. I really wasn't sure if I was going to get through this year, but I feel stronger than I have in a long time. I am praying more, praying in the Spirit more, studying more, and worshiping more.

Let me speak on prayer just a moment. We cannot expect God to answer our prayers if we use Him like a puppet on a string and only go to Him when we need things. Sometimes it can take a lifetime to see an answer to prayer come to pass. Our children must see us persevere and not give up. We do not serve a microwave "have it your way" God. I believe He wants to move in our lives where we can pray a prayer similar to the 60ish word prayer of Elijah and see fire come down from Heaven. But remember Elijah walked with God. He communed with Him because he loved God. I urge you to please don't wait until tragedy comes to your house to call on Him. Now is the time. Today is your day. He is waiting for you to invite Him into your life.

I have heard many powerful testimonies over the years. We all have a common theme. God came to the rescue.

Do you remember when He came to your rescue? What's holding you back? What is the excuse the enemy is using to keep you from just diving deep with Jesus? My heartache and pain can't compare to what so many others have endured. I think of Pastor Saheed who was captured and held in an Iranian prison for almost four years. We just heard of his release on January 16, 2016. He would write letters as encouragement to others, witnessing that God can keep His children even in the most unthinkable situations. I thought many times of his wife who knew the persecution Saheed faced. I had knots in my stomach, as if it was someone whom I loved with all my heart that was walking in his shoes. Many prayers went up for this man of God, and I was ever so thankful when I heard that he along with three other prisoners had been released.

There's much debate regarding why some go through more than others. Some would say it's the amount of sin in one's life. Job's so-called friends would taunt him. Eliphaz the Temanite[8] acknowledges that Job was a source of strength and encouragement to others in verse 3, but by verse 7 he turns around and tells Job the reason he suffers is because of the things he has done. Eliphaz states, "As I have observed, those who plow evil and those who sow trouble reap it," (Job 4:8). Eliphaz and Job's other friends did not know about the conversation that transpired between God and Satan earlier in Job 1:8 (NIV), when the Lord said to Satan, "Have you considered my servant Job? There is no one on earth like him: he is blameless and upright, a man who fears God and shuns evil." Don't let the enemy blame you. You know if you are walking upright before the Lord. If you are not, then allow God's correction to guide you to repentance.

[8] TOW Project. "Job's Friends Accuse Him of Doing Evil." *Theology of Work*. Retrieved from https://www.theologyofwork.org/old-testament/job/jobs-friends-blame-job-for-the-calamity-job-4-23/jobs-friends-accuse-him-of-doing-evil-job-4-23/

I do believe the Lord chastises or corrects his children. Hebrews 12:5-7,10 (NIV) tells us, "And you have forgotten the word of encouragement that addresses you as sons. 'My sons, do not make light the Lord's discipline and do not lose heart when he rebukes you, because the Lord disciplines those he loves, and he punishes everyone he accepts as a son.' Endure hardship as discipline; God is treating you as sons. If you are not disciplined, then you are illegitimate children and not true sons...God disciplines us for our good that we may share in his holiness."

There were definite times in my walk that I needed correction from the Lord. I still do. When we are walking close to Him, we can hear the still small voice of the Holy Spirit nudge us and convict us when we are not pleasing to Him. I pray that we all can hear that voice and instead of running from it, embrace His correction. God is not a mean Father with a hammer in His hand ready to beat us to the ground when we do something contrary to His word. He is a loving God who attempts first to gently get our attention. He will use the correct amount and measure of discipline necessary to get our attention and I believe age-appropriate discipline. If our hearts are towards Him, we will surrender to His authority. He is a gentleman and will not force our allegiance to Him. If we choose not to listen and heed his loving corrections, He will allow us to go out from under the umbrella of His protection. God created us to fellowship with Him and to worship Him because we want to, not because we are made to. We have been given the free will to do so.

I do not believe I can live any way I choose and still make it to Heaven. I don't believe once you're saved you're always saved unless you live out the Word. In Luke 9:62, "Jesus replied, 'No one who puts a hand to the plow and looks back is fit for service in the kingdom of God.'" Hebrews 10:26 (NIV) tells us that "if we deliberately keep on sinning after we have received the knowledge of the truth, no sacrifice for sins is left" and in verse 27, "but only a fearful expectation of judgment and of raging fire that will consume the enemies of God." Friends, He calls those who turn their backs on Him His enemies.

Friends, you don't serve God with passion one day and then find yourself not praying, not going to church, or not reading God's Word. It is a slow fade and you wake up wondering how this happened. Thanks be to God that He loves the prodigals and that He will leave the 99 to go after the one (Matthew 18:12). But again we are human beings with free will. It is a scary place when we no longer hear His voice. When He nudges and we ignore time and time again, our hearts become hardened. John 14:20 (NIV) states that "He has blinded their eyes and hardened their hearts, so they can neither see with their eyes."

I'd rather be wrong in this and have a desire to live a holy, consecrated life than to live a sinful life and be condemned to hell. He did not leave gray areas to justify our sins. If Jesus' sacrifice was enough to save me from my sins then friend, it is also powerful enough to keep me from sinning. My cry to everyone who reads this book: No matter what is happening in your life, **"CHOOSE LIFE SO THAT YOU AND YOUR CHILDREN MAY LIVE**," (Deuteronomy 30:19, NIV).

CHAPTER SIXTEEN

In the book of Matthew (5:45) while Jesus was teaching about revenge, He tells us that God causes the sun to rise on the evil and the good, and sends rain on the righteous and the unrighteous. He never taught that calamity was only for the sinner. In Luke chapter 13, Jesus is calling people to repentance. This was His sole purpose. He did not come to earth to die in vain. He came to set people like you and I free from the grips of hell. I like what the *Life Application Study Bible* says about calamity in verses 1-5:

> Pilate may have killed the Galileans, because he thought they were rebelling against Rome; those killed by the tower of Siloam may have been working for the Romans on the aqueduct there. The Pharisees, who were opposed to using force to deal with Rome, would have said that the Galileans killed by Pilate deserved to

die for rebelling. The Zealots, a group of anti-Roman terrorists, would have said the aqueduct workers deserved to die for cooperating. Jesus dismissed the idea that accidents or human cruelties were God's judgment on especially bad sinners. Neither Galileans nor the workers should be blamed for their calamities. Whether a person is killed in a tragic accident or miraculously survives is not a measure of righteousness. Everyone has to die. Jesus did not explain why some live and some die tragically; instead he pointed out to everyone's need for repentance. No matter how or when it occurs; death is not the end. Jesus promises that those who believe in him should not perish but have eternal life (John 3:16, NIV).[9]

God's promises are true. He will go with us through the storms of life. The

---

[9]"Luke 13 Study Notes." *Life Application Study Bible (NLT)*. Tyndale House Publishers, 2004.

devil would love to have us believe that if God loved us, He would never allow us to go through anything and that we would never experience pain or hardship. The Bible does not teach this. There are those who will never serve God because of this lie, and they will be separated from His presence for eternity. This burdens my soul. We live in a culture that has become desensitized by the constant negativity from news media. We see and hear of people dying in horrible ways every single day...but do we stop and think that another soul has just gone out into eternity.

Do you know you have a divine purpose? That individual you are working with that is struggling in their marriage, who may be a single mom, who is dealing with addictions, who is suffering from depression... do you realize you may be the very one that could rescue their soul from an eternal hell? We have allowed fear to keep us from speaking up for our Lord, for showing others that we can live a life devoted solely to God, and that He is able to help us in times of trouble. Psalm 46:1(KJV) says, "God is our refuge and strength an ever-present help in time of trouble."

Are you struggling with addictions today? Pastor preached on how sanctification is both instantaneous and progressive. I remember my husband telling me how he would lie in bed at night and cry because he just wanted to be able to sleep. He would do cocaine and it would keep him up. He had given his heart to Jesus at 9 years old. He remembers the love he had in his heart for Jesus. He was not surrounded by those who cultivated spiritual growth in his life and eventually grew away from God. He lived a heathen lifestyle. He was 29 when his heart started acting crazy. He was sitting in his "barn" when he asked God to come into his heart. He said this literally changed his heart beat. He decided one week after he gave his heart back to God that he would go "visit a lady." A sickness came on him quickly. He became pale and his heart began to flutter. God said to him, "Boy you will live for me or you will die without me." He high-tailed it out of there. He gets teary eyed when he talks about how the Lord had given him a vision of Heaven. He was at his friend's house, Richard Payne. They were talking about God and reading the Bible. He said to Richard, "I just want to live for God all the days of my life." On his way home, James told God, "Lord, I meant what I said back there. I want to live for you all the days of my life." Immediately after he said that, God showed him a vision of a street of gold with mansions on both sides that went all the way down. He heard God say to him, "One day James you will be here." God delivered hubby instantly from alcohol and drugs. He did not change his personality instantly and neither does He do that for you and I. This comes from a progressive walk with him by growing in the Word, going to church and having a deep intimate relationship with Jesus through prayer and worship.

Are you struggling with feeling lonely? Have you been betrayed by someone close to you? Do you long for someone's arms to draw you near to them? I must admit there have been times when I have felt the heavens shut, but I can assure you it was not because God is not who He says he is. God's love is an everlasting love. He wants a personal relationship with us, one where we can just go to him and say, "Daddy, I need you!!" When we surrender all to Him, that's when He can perform His complete work in us. I have been so guilty so many times trying to fix things on my own. I can really make a mess of things, ya know? This is a faith issue. I am asking God to help me in this area of my life. I have heard many others say as I have said, "I have faith for others and can believe God on their behalf, but I struggle with believing for myself."

This is why it is important to have Godly friends who you can talk to and who will pray for you when you are going through difficult times. Ecclesiastes 4:9-12 (NIV) says it best: "Two are better than one, because they have a good return for their work: If one falls down, his friend can help him up. But pity the man who falls and has no one to help him up! Also, if two lie down together, they will keep warm. But how can one keep warm alone? Though one may be overpowered, two can defend themselves. A cord of three strands is not quickly broken." Isolation is a tool of the enemy to cause us to feel we can go it alone. This can easily cause one to go into a state of depression. There are people who need you, who need your wisdom, who need your insight, and who need your friendship. Don't be selfish and self-serving, but let's go out and fulfill God's plan for our lives by influencing those He places in our path. I have to work on this, because as you have heard, my life has been constantly filled with struggles and this has been a major barrier to building strong friendships. I've purposed in my heart to do better with this, although it is completely out of my comfort zone.

There are so many I am praying for who are dealing with sickness, who have been imprisoned, who deal with struggles, bondages, chains and pain, who are experiencing divorce, abandonment, and addictions…the list goes on. I long to see a move of God across our land with signs and wonders, healings and deliverance before the trumpet sounds. I want to be a part of the last day's Holy Ghost movement. It will take dedication and commitment to prayer and a heart-felt relationship with my Savior.

Do you know the Peacekeeper today? If you have any doubt that He is who He says He is, I encourage you to ask Him to reveal Himself to you. I recently reminded Kayla as we grieve the loss of her cat that God sent to her 4 years ago. She doesn't understand why God didn't protect him. I don't have the answer, but I am reminded of what Job said, "the Lord gives and the

Lord takes away, blessed be the name of the Lord" (Job 1:21). Can you say that today? Can you say in whatever circumstances you are facing that God is who He says he is?

Maybe you don't know Jesus, will you consider making Him Lord of your life, and be the one to change your generation for Christ? How can anyone endure these things without God? I promise you I would not be here in my right mind without Him in my life. Listen, all the pain is worth it if on the other side of glory, we can spend eternity together. Have you broken the 10 Commandments like my husband and I have? If you have committed one sin the Bible says you are guilty of all and are in need of a Savior. (James 2:10) Don't wait for the "perfect time." Today is the day of salvation. I did not know how I was going to get out of the mess I was in when I surrendered my life to God, but He made a way. He gave me the chance to speak life to my family and I am forever thankful and blessed friends. If you are at place in your life where my mother once was, and you are not sure what to pray allow me to lead you in a prayer that will change the footsteps of your destiny.

Lord, I am a sinner. I am in need of a Savior. I confess my sins, and I turn from them. Please forgive me. I ask You to take the reins of my life and help me to serve You with my whole heart. I believe Jesus is the Son of God, and I want to spend eternity with You. I want to help others know You. Thank You for coming into my heart. In Jesus name, Amen.

If you prayed this prayer, I want to encourage you to find a church and get plugged in. Surround yourself with other believers. Spend time in prayer and in the Word of God. We serve an almighty God who knows exactly where you are, and He has the power to rescue you out of your situation. He is a way maker. He is the Lion of Judah. Let Him roar through you as you serve Him with your entire being and surrender all to Him.   I promise, YOU CAN MAKE IT!!

....

If this book has been an encouragement to you, or if you have considered surrendering your life to God, I want to know. Please take a few minutes and send an email to diana.jimison@gmail.com. My prayer is that you will run to Him and no other source for He is truly all we need.

www.ingramcontent.com/pod-product-compliance
Lightning Source LLC
Chambersburg PA
CBHW060921040426
42445CB00011B/723